MATTHEW R. LARSON *&* TIMOTHY D. KANOLD

BALANCING
the
EQUATION

A GUIDE TO SCHOOL MATHEMATICS FOR
EDUCATORS & PARENTS

Solution Tree | Press
a division of
Solution Tree

NATIONAL COUNCIL OF
TEACHERS OF MATHEMATICS

Mathematics
AT WORK™

555 North Morton Street
Bloomington, IN 47404
800.733.6786 (toll free) / 812.336.7700
FAX: 812.336.7790

email: info@solution-tree.com
solution-tree.com

Visit **go.solution-tree.com/MathematicsatWork** to download the free
reproducibles in this book.

Printed in the United States of America

20   19   18   17   16   1   2   3   4   5

FSC
www.fsc.org
MIX
Paper from
responsible sources
FSC® C011935

Library of Congress Cataloging-in-Publication Data
Names: Larson, Matthew R. | Kanold, Timothy D.
Title: Balancing the equation : a guide to school mathematics for educators
   and parents / Matthew R. Larson, Timothy D. Kanold.
Description: Bloomington, IN : Solution Tree Press, [2016] | Includes
   bibliographical references and index.
Identifiers: LCCN 2016007619 | ISBN 9781936763689 (perfect bound)
Subjects: LCSH: Mathematics--Study and teaching--Parent participation--United
   States. | Education--Parent participation--United States. |
   Teacher-student relationships--United States. | Parent-teacher
   relationships--United States.
Classification: LCC QA135.6 .L38 2016 | DDC 510.71/273--dc23 LC record available at
http://lccn.loc.gov/2016007619

Solution Tree
Jeffrey C. Jones, CEO
Edmund M. Ackerman, President

Solution Tree Press
President: Douglas M. Rife
Editorial Director: Tonya Maddox Cupp
Senior Acquisitions Editor: Amy Rubenstein
Managing Production Editor: Caroline Weiss
Senior Production Editor: Christine Hood
Copy Editor: Sarah Payne-Mills
Text and Cover Designer: Abigail Bowen
Compositor: Laura Kagemann

Acknowledgments

We owe a debt of gratitude to Solution Tree leaders Jeff Jones and Douglas Rife, who supported the vision for this book from the very beginning. It is not possible to create a labor of love, such as this book, without the sustained help and support of a remarkable team of editors: Christine Hood and Sarah Payne-Mills. Our thanks to both of them.

We also are grateful for all of our mathematics education colleagues who urged us to write this book for parents and for the benefit of K–12 educators dedicated to making mathematics important, meaningful, and relevant for all students.

We dedicate this book to you, the reader. To all of you who want what we have wanted our entire careers: to help our children and students be successful in learning the K–12 mathematics necessary to support great college and career choices.

Solution Tree Press would like to thank the following reviewers:

Vicky Armstrong
Director of Curriculum
Dinuba Unified School District
Dinuba, California

Robert Kaplinsky
Mathematics Coach
Downey Unified School District
Downey, California

Diana Kasbaum
Coordinator
Association of State Supervisors
   of Mathematics Presidential
   Awards for Excellence in
   Mathematics and Science
   Teaching
Windsor, Wisconsin

Donna Simpson Leak
Superintendent
Community Consolidated
   Schools District 168
Sauk Village, Illinois

Barbara Perez
Director of Mathematics
Clark County School District
Las Vegas, Nevada

Janice Richardson Plumblee
Associate Professor Emerita,
   Mathematics and Education
Elon University
Elon, North Carolina

Nick Resnick
Program Manager, Math
   in Common
California Education Partners
San Francisco, California

Sarah Schuhl
Senior Associate, Mathematics
   at Work™
Gresham, Oregon

Jeanne Spiller
Assistant Superintendent for
   Teaching and Learning
   Curriculum and Instruction
Kildeer Countryside
   Community Consolidated
   School District 96
Buffalo Grove, Illinois

Visit **go.solution-tree.com/MathematicsatWork**
to download the free reproducibles in this book.

Table of Contents

PART II

About the Authors

 **Matthew R. Larson, PhD,** is an award-winning educator and author who served as the K–12 mathematics curriculum specialist for Lincoln Public Schools in Nebraska for more than twenty years. He is the president of the National Council of Teachers of Mathematics (NCTM; 2016–2018). Dr. Larson has taught mathematics at the elementary through college levels and has held an honorary appointment as a visiting associate professor of mathematics education at Teachers College, Columbia University.

He is coauthor of several mathematics textbooks, professional books, and articles in mathematics education. A frequent keynote speaker at U.S. and state mathematics meetings, Dr. Larson's presentations are well known for their directness, humor, and application of research findings to practice.

Dr. Larson earned a bachelor's degree and doctorate from the University of Nebraska–Lincoln.

To learn more about Dr. Larson's work, visit his monthly *President's Messages* blog on the NCTM website (www.nctm.org).

 **Timothy D. Kanold, PhD,** is an award-winning educator, author, and consultant. He is former director of mathematics and science and served as superintendent of Adlai E. Stevenson High School District 125, a model professional learning community (PLC) district in Lincolnshire, Illinois.

Dr. Kanold is committed to equity and excellence for students, faculty, and school administrators. He conducts highly motivational professional development leadership seminars worldwide with a focus on turning school vision into realized action that creates greater equity for students through the effective delivery of PLCs for faculty and administrators. Dr. Kanold currently serves as the director of Mathematics at Work™, a comprehensive K–12 school improvement program to promote and improve student learning in mathematics.

He is past president of the National Council of Supervisors of Mathematics (NCSM) and coauthor of several best-selling mathematics textbooks since the late 1980s. He has served on writing commissions for NCTM and NCSM and has authored numerous articles and chapters on school leadership and development for education publications.

Dr. Kanold received the prestigious international 2010 Damen Award for outstanding contributions to the leadership field of education from Loyola University Chicago, the 1986 Presidential Award for Excellence in Mathematics and Science Teaching, and the 1994 Outstanding Administrator Award (from the Illinois State Board of Education). He serves as an adjunct faculty member for the graduate school at Loyola University Chicago.

Dr. Kanold earned a bachelor's degree in education and a master's degree in mathematics from Illinois State University. He completed a master's degree in educational administration at the University of Illinois and received a doctorate in educational leadership and counseling psychology from Loyola University Chicago.

To learn more about Dr. Kanold's work, visit his blog, *Turning Vision Into Action* (http://tkanold.turningvisionintoaction.net).

To book Matthew R. Larson or Timothy D. Kanold for professional development, contact pd@solution-tree.com.

Introduction

e·qui·lib·ri·um
A state in which opposing forces or influences are balanced.
—*NEW OXFORD AMERICAN DICTIONARY,*
THIRD EDITION

We love mathematics. We love students—all of the roughly fifty-four million going to school in the United States each year. We love and admire mathematics teachers. And we deeply appreciate the critical role that parents play in their children's education. We know it is every parent's desire for his or her child to succeed in learning mathematics. We also believe it is every educator's desire—teachers, administrators, teacher leaders, central office personnel, and school board members—to see each and every student in his or her school or school district succeed in learning K–12 mathematics. And yet, this goal of mathematics success for each student is often very difficult to achieve.

We are parents or relatives of parents; we have been mathematics teachers and have served as teacher leaders; and we have dedicated our entire professional lives in the service of K–12 mathematics education. We have witnessed student, parent, and teacher frustration, and we also have observed student, parent, and teacher joy when students effectively learn mathematics.

This is why it has been so hard for us to observe K–12 mathematics education under attack (Common Core or otherwise) by vitriolic rhetoric and a confusing lack of accurate information.

Why are we writing this book? It is our desire to provide information and insight that you can use to help you and your colleagues, friends, and relatives to better understand the answer to what should be a simple question: What do we want our students to know and be able to do, and how should they learn it as part of their K–12 mathematics education?

This book is for you, the educators: teachers, administrators, school board members, mathematics program leaders, instructional coaches, university professors—every individual responsible in some way for K–12 mathematics education.

This book is also for you, the parents. We use the term *parents* broadly to include grandparents, other family members, guardians, friends, and neighbors of the students in our communities. These individuals not only care about student success in mathematics but also may have questions about effective mathematics instruction and what is taking place in their local schools based on what they see or hear in the media.

Educators and parents can both effectively use this book. Educators may use this book as a tool to deepen their understanding of effective mathematics instruction and discuss it with their colleagues in professional development settings or book studies. They may recommend the book to parents or use it with them directly to help parents better understand the outcomes and instructional strategies for mathematics learning and why these outcomes and strategies are important. Finally, concerned parents may read this book on their own to deepen their understanding of mathematics education and recommend it to their friends and neighbors who have questions about the mathematics education taking place in their schools.

We hope this book will serve you well as you deepen your understanding of mathematics education and influence your friends, fellow parents, or professional colleagues to help ensure all students have access to high-quality instruction in mathematics.

The Purpose of This Book

We initially started writing this book to clarify misunderstandings regarding the Common Core State Standards (CCSS), which the state governors commissioned in April 2009 (National Governors Association Center for Best Practices [NGA], 2009). However, it became much more than that for us. We want to ensure that the hope and promise for improving K–12 mathematics teaching and learning, which characterized the first few years after 2010, is not lost on students.

We wrote this book with future high school graduates in mind, those living in your neighborhoods or on your street. We do not want those students, and every current or future graduating class of students around them, to regress to a mathematics curriculum from the 1980s and early 1990s. Many of the mathematics curricula of that era, with respect to instructional approach, content, and assessment practices, simply failed to represent the needed state of equilibrium, and as a result, consistently failed to serve students well enough.

We define *equilibrium* in mathematics education as a program that has "balanced the equation" in its instructional approach to blending procedural fluency, conceptual understanding, and problem solving—an approach in which students learn *how* to do mathematics, *why* mathematics works, and *when* to apply mathematics. A program that has "balanced the equation" not only approaches *how*, *why*, and *when* with equal intensity, but also views them as mutually supportive and necessary to mathematical literacy. This equilibrium, or balance, with respect to mathematics education, will be fully defined in chapter 4.

> *A program that has "balanced the equation" not only approaches how, why, and when with equal intensity, but also views them as mutually supportive and necessary to mathematical literacy.*

Our purpose is to refocus the mathematics education discussion in which educators and parents engage with each other: your friends, neighbors, colleagues, and other local school district educators. Your conversations must move away from misinformation, misguided rhetoric, and extremes (often the stuff that grabs the headlines or characterizes tweets and Facebook and Instagram posts) that do nothing to improve mathematics teaching and learning in U.S. classrooms. Instead, we propose moving toward a discussion of the elements of mathematics instruction that result in significant increases in student learning.

Our purpose is to provide both educators *and* parents with accurate information and research that support the future learning of our students. We seek to do the following.

- Explain why we need to raise our expectations for effective teaching and learning of mathematics *immediately*

- Show how debates in mathematics education have a long history, are somewhat cyclical, and have only served to foster a state of near continual disequilibrium and dysfunction toward the successful teaching and learning of K–12 mathematics

- Explain why parents must expect and support effective mathematics teaching and learning for their children during this era of mathematics reform—the CCSS initiative era

- Define mathematical literacy and illustrate the effective elements of great mathematics instruction that leads to improved student learning

- Outline how educators *and* parents can help each child successfully learn mathematics and offer actions they can take to support improved mathematics teaching and learning

Evidence indicates that most people in the United States get their information about education and schools from family and friends—not from research literature or experts (West, Whitehurst, & Dionne, 2011). So although this is not a research or academic book per se, we cite some of the peer-reviewed research and literature that support the points we make. We do not rely on mere opinion.

Peer-reviewed research is the most credible evidence—well above opinions often read in someone's blog or tweets or stories that appear in the media—because prior to publication, individuals of similar expertise review the work. The peer-review process helps ensure high standards of quality, and the arguments in this book are based on peer-reviewed literature. We present for you not opinions, but facts. We cite the research so you know with confidence that our arguments are based both on evidence of current U.S. student achievement and on the research-informed actions educators and parents are taking that make a significant difference for K–12 learning in every school community.

An Overview of the Book

Part I of this book consists of chapters 1–3. We wrote these chapters primarily for educators. However, we hope that parents also will find it informative when thinking about why the mathematics education their children receive should be different from their own experiences growing up. We highlight information for parents in these three chapters in feature boxes; we believe this information will help parents guide their children in their journey through mathematics.

Chapter 1 discusses why change is necessary, specifically why the status quo with respect to much of mathematics teaching and learning is currently insufficient—that is, not nearly good enough for *all* of those fifty-four million students.

Chapter 2 offers a brief history of mathematics education to demonstrate that debates about this topic have a long history—a history cycle of disequilibrium between two opposing forces. This disequilibrium must end if we hope to ever seriously improve mathematics teaching and learning for every student.

Chapter 3 presents the Common Core debate. We separate the debate about standards *testing* (very controversial in some parts of the country) from the actual implementation of *content* and *process* standards (less controversial but more widely misinterpreted). We help focus the debate on facts and research, not opinion and misinformation, and we show that the correct expectation for K–12 mathematics curriculum, instruction, and assessment should be the balanced pursuit of a *state of equilibrium*. By *equilibrium*, we do not mean to imply that effective mathematics programs are at rest; rather, that within effective mathematics programs, the beliefs (or views) of traditionally opposing forces are *balanced*.

> *We help focus the debate on facts and research, not opinion and misinformation.*

Part II of this book includes chapters 4 and 5, which we wrote primarily as a guide for parents and the expectations they should advocate for regarding K–12 mathematics teaching and learning in their children's schools. However, these two chapters also serve as a guide for educators to help check the quality of their professional work for effective mathematics teaching and learning. In these two chapters, we provide feature boxes to inform and guide educators.

Chapter 4 defines mathematical literacy, highlights elements of mathematics programs that are in a state of equilibrium, and describes essential features of effective mathematics instruction—the instructional strategies parents should expect their child's classroom teachers to employ. These are the strategies teachers try to pursue, and local administrators and school board members expect, in order to gain significant increases in student learning and success in mathematics.

Chapter 5 offers suggestions on how parents can help their children learn mathematics at home and at school and how educators can support every parent in this pursuit.

We wrote the epilogue to both educators and parents. It offers our reflections on why common standards are necessary to prevent inequity and why the instruction mathematics educators and parents expect students to receive must change and why that change is so challenging to implement. In addition, we offer actions educators and parents can take to improve mathematics learning outcomes for all students. The hope is that whether students graduate from high school and walk across that stage in 2020 or 2028 or 2034 or beyond, the efforts educators and parents make today to improve mathematics education will result in better learning opportunities for every student. Ready? Let's go!

PART I

The primary audience for part I is educators. However, we believe there is much in part I that is of interest to parents as they seek to understand the need to change how we have traditionally taught mathematics, the impact of the history of mathematics education in the United States and how it influences education debates, why common standards are so important, and why mathematics educators must expect more of their students.

We hope the following chapters will guide educators in evaluating the quality of their mathematics programs and practices. Parents will find numerous feature boxes titled "Reflections for Parents." They can use this information to enhance their personal knowledge development, in discussions with other parents, or for participation in group study such as PTA meetings or a school mathematics task force.

Chapter 1

Why Mathematics Education Needs to Improve

We are systematically underestimating what our kids can do in math.

—AMANDA RIPLEY,
INVESTIGATIVE JOURNALIST AND AUTHOR

Since the 1990s, efforts to improve mathematics teaching and learning have focused on state adoption and implementation of increasingly more rigorous K–12 mathematics standards. These state standards represent the guaranteed and viable curriculum that every student should learn—what we expect students to know and be able to do in each grade level and course. In addition, each state implemented accountability measures attached to attainment of those standards.

The Era of Standards-Based Reform

The standards movement was kick-started by the National Council of Teachers of Mathematics (NCTM) in 1989, when it published *Curriculum and Evaluation Standards for School Mathematics*. This document and the subsequent edition, *Principles and Standards for School Mathematics* (NCTM, 2000), as well as *Curriculum Focal Points for Prekindergarten Through Grade 8 Mathematics* (NCTM, 2006), served as the blueprints for various state mathematics standards produced over a two-decade period beginning in the early 1990s. NCTM presented a new sense of rigor in terms of both the *what* and the *how* of learning school mathematics.

Throughout this book, when we use the term *rigor*, we do not simply mean the level of difficulty of the mathematics students must learn. We are referring to the level and complexity of *reasoning* in which students are required to engage to solve a problem (Kanold, Briars, & Fennell, 2012). At the upper end of rigor, students might be required to explain their thinking, use evidence, apply mathematics to a new situation, or make a plan to solve a problem over an extended period of time (Smith & Stein, 2012).

It is worth pausing for a moment to examine whether or not these newer mathematics standards have worked to improve student learning. The short response is yes and no.

Beginning in the 1990s and continuing through the 2010s, new and more rigorous state mathematics standards, including the states adopting the CCSS for mathematics, were successively implemented. Thus, it is worth pausing for a moment to examine whether or not these newer mathematics standards have worked to improve student learning. The short response is *yes* and *no*.

The State of Student Mathematics Achievement: Good News

So, how are the fifty-four million K–12 students enrolled in school doing during the era of mathematics reform, since the early 1990s? One place you can look for evidence of improved learning is the National Assessment of Educational Progress (NAEP). NAEP is the largest U.S. organization that provides a continual assessment of what U.S. students know and can do. NAEP was measuring student performance in mathematics when you were in school as well.

The National Center for Education Statistics (NCES), located within the U.S. Department of Education's Institute of Education Sciences, administers the same NAEP assessment in every state, making it significantly different from the patchwork quilt of assessments states under No Child Left Behind (NCLB) have administered since 2002. (See pages 40–41 for a more complete explanation of NCLB.) Under NCLB, each state set its own standards, made its own test, and set its own passing score, making the results incomparable (Bandeira de Mello, Bohrnstedt, Blankenship, & Sherman, 2015). The NAEP assessments provide valid and reliable measures of student progress over time (Daro, Hughes, & Stancavage, 2015). The main NAEP assessments are administered in the fourth, eighth, and twelfth grades. Mathematics and reading are assessed every two years.

Although one should cautiously interpret NAEP scores—establishing causality between NAEP scores and particular policies can be difficult (Loveless, 2013)—it is still worth asking, "What are the NAEP mathematics results over the period of standards-based reform, since 1990?"

Looking at scores over a number of years (1990 to 2015) versus two adjacent assessment periods (2013 to 2015) is the most valid way to interpret scores because the tests are designed to measure student performance over time (Daro et al., 2015). Since 1990, at both the elementary and middle school levels, the long-term trend in NAEP scores has been positive (NCES, 2015). In fact, since 2003, NAEP scores in all fifty states have improved more than would be expected based on demographic shifts between 2003 and 2013 (Chingos, 2015). In 2015, both fourth-grade and eighth-grade mathematics achievement declined slightly from all-time high scores in 2013 (by one and two points respectively) but were significantly higher than in 1990 (NCES, 2015).

Small declines between 2013 and 2015 could have a variety of causes, but this might be due to the alignment of NAEP with the CCSS. While the 2015 NAEP mathematics framework is relatively well aligned with the Common Core (for example, 79 percent of the NAEP items at grade 4 were matched to the Common Core at grade 4 or below, and 87 percent of the NAEP items at grade 8 were matched to the Common Core at grade 8 or below), there are still differences between it and the CCSS for mathematics (Daro et al., 2015).

Despite the small decline in scores in 2015, the overall trend is positive, and students have made significant progress since 1990 at both the elementary and middle school levels.

Researchers have suggested that because the NAEP mathematics framework has not been updated since 2005, and U.S. mathematics standards have shifted over that same time period (specifically regarding the emphasis on various topics taught in certain grades), it is time for the NAEP mathematics framework to be reviewed and updated to reflect the new standards (Daro et al., 2015).

In summary, despite the small decline in scores in 2015, the overall trend is positive, and students have made significant progress since 1990 at both the elementary and middle school levels.

- In 2015, 40 percent of fourth graders scored proficient or above on the NAEP, rising from 13 percent in 1990—the bulk of the time period covered by standards-based mathematics reform (NCES, 2015).

- In 2015, 33 percent of eighth graders scored proficient or above on the NAEP, rising from 15 percent in 1990—the bulk of the time period covered by standards-based mathematics reform (NCES, 2015).

- Perhaps most significant, based on the NAEP long-term trend assessment (initiated in 1973), fourth graders and eighth graders in 2012 (the last time assessment results were available) were performing at a significantly higher level than their parents and grandparents did in mathematics (Dossey, Halvorsen, & McCrone, in press).

There is similar good news with respect to mathematics achievement at the high school level. The mean SAT mathematics score increased between 1990 and 2015, with a record number of test takers in 2015 (College Board, 2015a). Similarly, the mean ACT mathematics score increased between 1990 and 2015, with a record number of test takers in 2015 (ACT, 2015). In addition, the number of students taking the advanced placement (AP) calculus and AP statistics examinations reached a record high in 2014 (College Board, 2014).

The national high school graduation rate reached a record high of 82.3 percent for the class of 2014 (Ujifusa, 2015), and for the fourth year in a row, it remained on pace to meet the 90 percent goal by the class of 2020.

The national high school graduation rate reached a record high of 82.3 percent for the class of 2014 (Ujifusa, 2015), and for the fourth year in a row, it remained on pace to meet the 90 percent goal by the class of 2020 (America's Promise Alliance, 2015). Combine these results with the highest parent satisfaction rates in the history of the Gallup Poll about the quality of education in 2014 (Riffkin, 2014), and you might wonder, "What is the problem then?"

We do not mean for this discussion of assessment results to be interpreted as the only lens through which to examine mathematics education; that is, through a focus on achievement only. We agree with researchers who argue that mathematics learning outcomes also must be viewed through the lens of experience. Learning outcomes are in large part a function of how students experience mathematics learning, participate, and are motivated by their individual agencies and identities (Martin, 2007). Yet, having acknowledged this limitation, the evidence of student learning on a national scale is not all together good either.

The State of Student Mathematics Achievement: Bad News

With all of this good news regarding student mathematics achievement—near historic highs for certain grade levels by some measures—you might reasonably ask, "Why is change necessary?" Simple: because not all the news is good, and even the good news hides some ugly realities.

* While fourth-grade and eighth-grade mathematics achievement (as measured by the NAEP) has significantly improved since 1990, *less than half of all students are proficient* (NCES, 2015). Yes, the percentage of students who are proficient has more than tripled for fourth grade and more than doubled for eighth grade over the period of standards-based reform, but it is still less than half.

* While the difference in mean NAEP mathematics scores between fourth-grade (see figure 1.1, page 14) and eighth-grade (see figure 1.2, page 15) white and African American students and fourth-grade (see figure 1.3, page 16) and eighth-grade (see figure 1.4, page 17) white and Latino students has narrowed since 1990, significant learning differentials remain (NCES, 2015). You can visit **go.solution-tree.com/MathematicsatWork** to download free reproducibles of figures 1.1–1.4.

* Mean NAEP scores for high school students have been essentially flat since 1973 (NCES, 2013).

* Fewer than 50 percent of U.S. high school graduates in 2015 were considered ready for college-level mathematics work, as measured by their ACT mathematics scores (ACT, 2015).

* U.S. high school students' performance on international assessments, particularly assessments that emphasize the ability to apply and use mathematics, ranks below the international mean (average) and declined between 2009 and 2012 (Organisation for Economic Co-operation and Development [OECD], 2014).

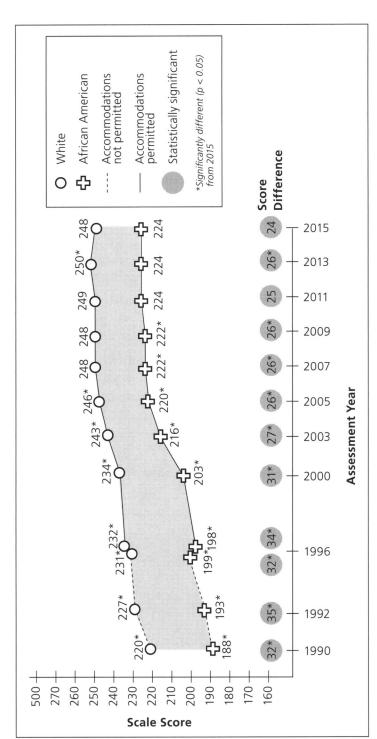

Figure 1.1: Trend in fourth-grade NAEP average scores and score gaps between white and African American students 1990–2015.

Source: NCES, 2015. Used with permission from the U.S. Department of Education, Institute of Education Sciences, National Center for Education Statistics, National Assessment of Educational Progress, 2009 Mathematics Assessment.

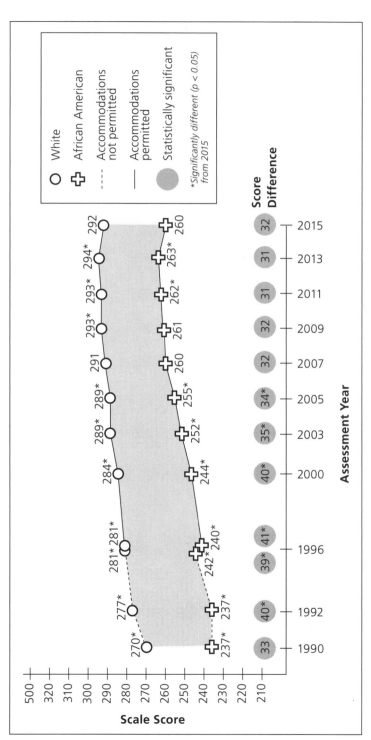

Figure 1.2: Trend in eighth-grade NAEP average scores and score gaps between white and African American students 1990–2015.

Source: NCES, 2015. Used with permission from the U.S. Department of Education, Institute of Education Sciences, National Center for Education Statistics, National Assessment of Educational Progress, 2009 Mathematics Assessment.

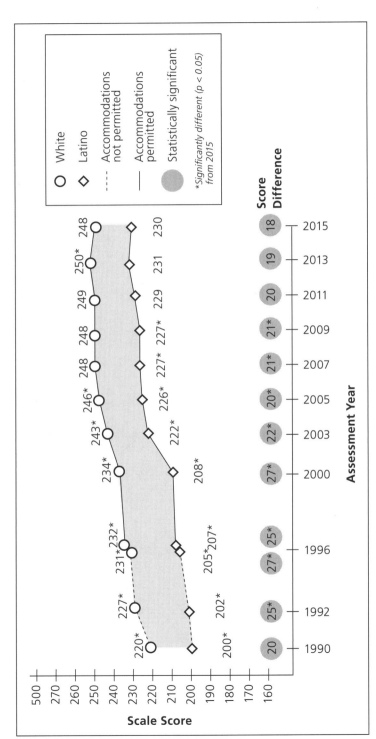

Source: NCES, 2015. Used with permission from the U.S. Department of Education, Institute of Education Sciences, National Center for Education Statistics, National Assessment of Educational Progress, 2009 Mathematics Assessment.

Figure 1.3: Trend in fourth-grade NAEP average scores and score gaps between white and Latino students 1990–2015.

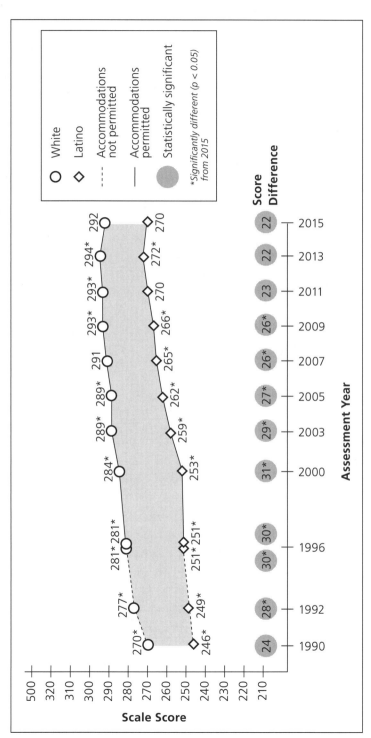

Figure 1.4: Trend in eighth-grade NAEP average scores and score gaps between white and Latino students 1990–2015.

Source: NCES, 2015. Used with permission from the U.S. Department of Education, Institute of Education Sciences, National Center for Education Statistics, National Assessment of Educational Progress, 2009 Mathematics Assessment.

- U.S. millennials, the generation born after 1980, have numeracy skills that rank last among twenty-three participating countries. This means that young adults in the United States experience significant difficulty when faced with solving problems that require several steps, the choice of problem-solving strategies, or interpreting and identifying relevant information (Goodman, Sands, & Coley, 2015).

U.S. student achievement in mathematics can be summarized as follows: U.S. students have made significant learning gains in mathematics since 1990. However, U.S. student proficiency in mathematics is insufficient; unacceptable learning differentials remain between different demographic groups in the United States. U.S. student achievement lags behind many international peers, and there is evidence that young adults have difficulty applying mathematical skills. In other words, while progress has been made, more work needs to be done. In addition, there is evidence that states have set too low a standard for assessing student proficiency in mathematics.

The Proficiency Bar: Ending Disparity

The evidence for lowering the bar for student proficiency shows in the discrepancy between the percent of students reported proficient on the NAEP and the percentage of students reported proficient by individual states (Achieve, 2015). Of the forty-three states and the District of Columbia included in the comparison study at the eighth-grade level in 2013–2014, only New York and Massachusetts reported a lower level of proficiency on their state mathematics test than they reported on the NAEP (Achieve, 2015). This means that New York and Massachusetts set relatively high standards for proficiency. For the remaining states and the District of Columbia, the average discrepancy was more than twenty-three points.

U.S. student achievement lags behind many international peers, and there is evidence that young adults have difficulty applying mathematical skills.

In 2013, for example, only five states (North Carolina, Wisconsin, New York, Massachusetts, and Texas) had a state standard for proficient performance in fourth-grade mathematics equivalent to the NAEP standard for proficient performance (Bandeira de Mello et al., 2015). Every other state's targets for proficiency on its state assessment were lower than the NAEP targets for proficiency and resulted in somewhat to significantly higher state-reported rates of mathematics proficiency. At the eighth-grade level, the results in 2013 were even more disappointing: only three states (North Carolina, Texas, and New York) had standards that met the NAEP proficiency levels (Bandeira de Mello et al., 2015).

An American Institutes for Research (AIR) report compares the mathematics proficiency targets in each state with the international benchmark used in the Trends in International Mathematics and Science Study (TIMSS; Phillips, 2010). (See Larson & Leinwand, 2013a, 2013b, and 2013c for a more detailed description.) Comparing state proficiency targets with international benchmarks is informative, because one criterion for the development of the CCSS for mathematics was that they be internationally benchmarked for proficiency levels.

The AIR report compares mathematics proficiency, as states under the requirements of NCLB reported in 2007, to an estimate of the percentage of students who would have met proficiency targets if the states had used an internationally benchmarked standard. At the eighth-grade level, the overall state mathematics proficiency rate would have dropped from 62 percent proficient to 29 percent proficient, and it would have dropped in each of the forty-eight states included in the study, with the exception of Massachusetts and South Carolina (Phillips, 2010). At the elementary level, the results are similar: the mean (average) fourth-grade state mathematics proficiency rate would have dropped from 72 to 39 percent, and it would have dropped in each of the forty-eight states included in the study, with the exception of Massachusetts (Phillips, 2010).

Comparing state proficiency targets with international benchmarks is informative, because one criterion for the development of the CCSS for mathematics was that they be internationally benchmarked for proficiency levels.

Reflections for **Parents**

Why were state mathematics test results so good during the NCLB era? Prior to 2015, with the older state mathematics tests students took each spring, you likely received results indicating your child was proficient in mathematics, which was good news. However, if you lived in a state that administered newer mathematics tests in the spring of 2015, which are considered more rigorous, you may have received different news (a lower score performance) regarding your child's proficiency in mathematics. Does this mean instruction in your child's school got worse? Are the new standards "bad," and is your child no longer learning as much? The answer to both questions is almost certainly *no!*

During the NCLB era, nearly all states set lower proficiency standards for student performance on the state tests. This meant that the mathematics standards themselves were more robust (a higher bar), but the testing of the standards had a much lower expectation for student performance and proficiency (a much lower bar). In the post-NCLB era, we continue to set the bar high for mathematic standards and state testing of those standards.

Low State Testing Expectations: A Critical Flaw

So here is the critical issue, no matter how difficult it is to accept: most states set relatively low mathematics testing performance standards with their state tests during the NCLB era (beginning in 2002 and then for more than a decade). The proficiency rates reported based on those tests did not adequately reflect what students need to know and be able to do in mathematics to compete internationally (Phillips, 2010).

This became a critical flaw in a high-skilled information economy in which students increasingly have to compete internationally for jobs (Friedman, 2005). A wide variety of jobs and careers use mathematical skills (National Research Council [NRC], 2012b), and acquisition of mathematical skills is linked to future earnings.

Stanford University professor Linda Darling-Hammond (2006, 2010) writes eloquently regarding the fact that the U.S. economy can no longer absorb unskilled workers at middle-class wages, and unless we give all students the skills they need to succeed in a knowledge-based economy, our societal infrastructure will be at risk. A Georgetown University Center on Education and the Workforce report (Carnevale, Cheah, & Hanson, 2015) reinforces Darling-Hammond's (2006, 2010) point: the median entry-level salary for college-educated STEM (science, technology, engineering, and mathematics) majors is the highest of major groups and nearly twice that of high school graduates. In addition, STEM majors experience the largest wage growth over the course of their careers (Carnevale et al., 2015).

In other words, state mathematics proficiency rates based on the old state test expectations inflated students' true level of mathematical understanding when measured against an international performance standard that *defines mathematical literacy in terms of understanding, procedural skill, and the ability to solve problems.* This coincides with mathematical skills becoming increasingly valuable in the workplace.

Here is the bottom line: the results of most state mathematics tests simply misled the public concerning whether or not students were truly proficient in mathematics (Achieve, 2015). We must accept this uncomfortable fact. The problem isn't the new mathematics content standards. The problem isn't testing in general or even the new state tests (even though they can and will be improved). The problem is that the majority of the old state tests had a lower proficiency bar of expectations. The results may have made us feel good, but the results weren't an honest assessment of what students should know and be able do in mathematics.

> *The problem is that the majority of the old state tests had a lower proficiency bar of expectations.*

The New Normal: We Need to Expect More

Adopting higher mathematics performance standards is essential if we want to give students the opportunity to learn the mathematics they need to become productive members of society, competing in a global economy that requires higher-level mathematics skills.

As results on new state assessments (for example, Smarter Balanced) were released in fall 2015, some states reported lower levels of proficiency in mathematics as compared to older state tests (Leal, 2015). Matthew Larson and Steven Leinwand (2013c) argue that lower test scores on new state tests are to be expected. They recommend the following with respect to interpreting the test results for your state and/or school district on the new assessments.

- Don't make comparisons to past scores on state assessments. Results on assessments reflect the performance on assessments set to a higher performance standard. This is a more realistic baseline of student achievement.

- Any decrease in your student's proficiency is most likely due to a change in the performance standard expectations (not a decrease in instructional effectiveness).

- Improvement under changed standards and assessments takes time. Meaningful improvement in teaching and learning is a complex endeavor.

Raising expectations and learning outcomes requires difficult choices in schools—choices that are not always popular. For example, a school district familiar to one of the authors of this book decided to eliminate one of two daily recesses at the elementary level in order to create more instructional time. By eliminating one daily recess and restructuring other parts of the day, the district was able to create an additional thirty minutes of daily mathematics instruction that could be utilized to support students who were struggling as well as provide enrichment to students experiencing success.

Reflections for Parents

What does this mean for your expectations? You should hold your children "to the highest standards that push them out of their comfort zones" (Friedman & Mandelbaum, 2011, p. 124). Unless your child engages in meaningful mathematics practice, both inside *and outside* of school, the goals of improved student learning and demonstrations of higher mathematics achievement are not possible. Thus, we strongly encourage you to support your child's school as it implements research-informed instructional practices and curriculum (print or digital textbooks) that increase the likelihood of *all* students—including your child—succeeding in mathematics during school and during mathematics practice at home.

In some of the district's elementary schools, parents were upset about the loss of one fifteen-minute recess. A small group of concerned parents started a grassroots campaign to reinstate the second recess. Parents tried to generate opposition to the new policy by using Facebook, calling central office administrators and school board members, contacting the local newspaper, and repeatedly expressing concerns to building principals—going so far, in some cases, as to stand on the playground and time the length of recess.

Our point here isn't that recess is bad. We believe students need physical activity and movement—and recess remained in this school district's daily schedule. What is significant is that this district maintained its revised time allotments despite the opposition. Ultimately, the result of increasing the amount of time devoted to focused mathematics instruction contributed to improving the district's performance on the state mathematics test at all elementary grade levels. As a result of the demonstrated improvement in learning, the vast majority of the community eventually accepted the loss of one recess.

The point of sharing this story is that change, nearly any change, is hard. We'll explain why changing mathematics instruction is particularly challenging, but the important point is that change, even though it may at times be uncomfortable, is necessary if our students are to be successful in mathematics, be prepared for college and the world of work, and have a full array of career opportunities available to them.

Although student mathematics achievement has improved over the era of standards-based mathematics reform, particularly at the elementary and middle school levels, the following is also true.

- Mathematics achievement is still relatively low in the United States, as measured by the NAEP (NCES, 2015).

- U.S. student mathematics achievement is below average and declining in an international context (OECD, 2014).

- Within the United States, unacceptable learning differentials based on race and economic status continue to exist (NCES, 2015). These differentials contribute to the widening economic and social gaps that threaten the social fabric of U.S. democracy (Darling-Hammond, 2006, 2010).

Consequently, mathematics instruction and expectations for students, educators, and parents in the United States *must* be improved and raised. The state of learning simply does not work for all students or even well enough for most students. We must confront the reality that to raise the mathematics achievement of U.S. students, teachers, school leaders, *and parents* must have the courage to accept that current achievement, while improving, is too low and educational opportunities too unequal. It's time to break the cycle of the past and demand and support the implementation of higher standards, more rigorous assessments, and research-informed instructional and education practices that build the mathematical identity and agency of all students—particularly traditionally marginalized students (Aguirre, Mayfield-Ingram, & Martin, 2013). This means seeking an equilibrium point with your school's mathematics program and embracing balance as the *new normal*.

It's time to break the cycle of the past and demand and support the implementation of higher standards, more rigorous assessments, and research-informed instructional and education practices that build the mathematical identity and agency of all students.

In chapter 2, we outline the concerns about mathematics education. The issues in mathematics education are recurrent, but that recurrence must end in order to ensure that high school graduates are college and career ready.

Questions for Reflection

Reflecting on your reading is an opportunity to evaluate and deepen your understanding, gain additional insight, and apply what you have read to your own specific context (Costa & Kallick, 2008). Whether you are an educator or parent, we encourage you to use these questions for personal reflection or to prompt discussion with colleagues and friends if you are reading the book together with the goal of understanding and improving mathematics learning in your local schools.

Questions for Educators

1. How are mathematics data and achievement shared in your local school, district, and state? Do you know how students in your school are performing in mathematics as compared to other students at the national level?

2. Are all students in your school achieving at high levels? Which student groups aren't performing to their potential? What instructional modifications and supports might you provide? What professional development do teachers need in order to build positive mathematical identities for all students?

3. What is your state's performance on the NAEP in mathematics? How does that performance compare to performance on the state mathematics test? Does your school provide this information to all parents?

Questions for Parents

1. Do you think expectations for mathematics achievement are high enough in your child's school? What can you do to support higher expectations for mathematics in your school?

2. If some parents in your child's school do not support increased expectations for mathematics, how would you communicate to those parents the need to raise mathematics performance standards for every student?

3. Are you surprised that, by some measures, mathematics achievement in the United States is the highest it has ever been? Do you think other parents and adults in your community are aware of the progress that has been made since standards-based reforms were implemented in the 1990s? How might you communicate this information to them?

Chapter 2

A Brief History of Mathematics Education

The issues in mathematics education tend to endure, to change slowly if at all.

—PHILIP S. JONES AND ARTHUR F. COXFORD,
EDITORS, *THE HISTORY OF MATHEMATICS
EDUCATION IN THE UNITED STATES AND CANADA*

A brief history of mathematics education since 1788 illustrates the recurrent underpinnings of the debates in mathematics education. As Christopher Phillips (2015) points out, these issues are "cyclical and seemingly intractable" (p. 20). Table 2.1 (pages 28–29) outlines select major events in the history of mathematics education discussed in this chapter, including some of the intractable issues since 1788.

The two most persistent questions in mathematics education have been and continue to be the following (Jones & Coxford, 1970).

1. What should be the nature of mathematics that students learn—facts, skills, and procedures, or concepts and understanding?

2. How should students learn mathematics— teacher directed with a focus on memorization, or student centered through reasoning and discovery?

The shaded rows in table 2.1 reflect the events and time periods that emphasized skills, procedures, direct teacher instruction, and student memorization. The unshaded rows reflect the events and time periods

Table 2.1: Major Events in U.S. Mathematics Education History

Date or Period	Publication or Era	Emphasis or Issue
1788	Publication of Nicolas Pike's *Arithmetic*	This book establishes the dominant U.S. mathematics teaching script: direct instruction, rules, examples, memorization, and skill practice.
1821	Publication of Warren Colburn's *An Arithmetic on the Plan of Pestalozzi*	This book emphasizes reasoning and understanding: students discover rules through structured investigation with hands-on materials.
1832	Publication of P. E. Bates Botham's *The Common School Arithmetic*	This book emphasizes direct instruction, memorization, and skill practice.
1892	Committee of Ten report	This report establishes the traditional high school sequence of algebra, geometry, and advanced algebra as separate courses.
Early 1900s	University of Chicago reform effort	This effort seeks to unify the secondary mathematics curriculum.
1910–1940s	Progressive education era	This era establishes tracking (academic and vocational mathematics courses) as high schools serve larger numbers of students.
1922	Publication of Edward L. Thorndike's *The Psychology of Arithmetic*	This book emphasizes extensive practice of isolated skills.
1930s	William Brownell's meaning theory	This theory emphasizes quantitative reasoning.
1959	Commission on Mathematics of the College Entrance Examination Board (CEEB)	This commission recommends that school curricula be organized around concepts, structures, and reasoning processes.

Date or Period	Publication or Era	Emphasis or Issue
1960s	New math	These concepts emphasize mathematical structure, reasoning, and understanding.
1970s–1980s	Back to the basics	These concepts emphasize direct instruction and skills practice.
1980	Publication of NCTM's *An Agenda for Action*	This publication emphasizes problem solving as driving instruction and the focus of the curriculum.
1989	Publication of NCTM's *Curriculum and Evaluation Standards for School Mathematics*	This publication establishes the first set of voluntary national content standards in any subject and emphasizes understanding and reasoning.
1990s and 2000s	Standards-based school reform	During this reform, states adopt their own mathematics standards based on NCTM standards of 1989 and 2000.
2000	Publication of NCTM's *Principles and Standards for School Mathematics*	In this publication, NCTM updates the 1989 publication and emphasizes mathematics learning as consisting of both process and content.
2001	NCLB	Federal legislation (reauthorization of the 1965 Elementary and Secondary Education Act [ESEA]) requires the adoption of both state content standards and state assessment of those standards with accountability requirements.
2001	Publication of the NRC's *Adding It Up*	This publication summarizes research at the time on K–8 mathematics learning and defines mathematical proficiency as multidimensional.
2008	Publication of the *National Mathematics Advisory Panel Report*	This report aims to end the "math wars."
2010	Publication of *The Common Core State Standards for Mathematics*	This publication emphasizes both skill development *and* student understanding, reasoning, and problem solving.
2015	CCSS assessments administered for the first time	These assessments result in serious pushback as well as emergence of the curriculum associated with the Common Core.

that emphasized conceptual understanding, student reasoning, more student engagement, and in some cases, student discovery or structured investigations of mathematical concepts.

However, it is important to note that reform approaches to mathematics education (for example, those emphasizing conceptual understanding and more student engagement in the learning process) never dominated classroom instruction during these eras. Leading mathematics educators and policy groups discussed and advocated for reforms, but these reforms were seldom widely adopted. As Jeremy Kilpatrick (2011) eloquently states, when you consider the history of school mathematics, there is often

> a lot of surface change going on at the top, whereas down at the bottom, where the curriculum really lives in classrooms, teaching and learning are unchanged or relatively unchanged. . . . The surface of the curricular ocean may sometimes appear to have been swept by a tsunami, but at the depths, life goes on much as before. (p. 9)

The "gravitational pull" of the traditional approach to mathematics education is very difficult to overcome.

How teachers, school leaders, and parents answer these two questions generally defines the two sides of nearly every debate in mathematics education. The answers to these questions likely determine whether one supports or opposes the CCSS for mathematics. The two differing perspectives on how best to answer these questions are illustrated in the texts, publications, and events presented in table 2.1, as discussed in the following section.

Mathematics Education in Early America: The Debate Emerges

In early colonial America, mathematics wasn't even a subject for young children beyond an expectation that they could write numbers and rote count (DeVault & Weaver, 1970). However, as business grew in the colonies, the need for more citizens to be able to perform simple arithmetic increased, and eventually, schools added arithmetic to the required subjects of religion, reading, and writing. Arithmetic was first required in Massachusetts and New Hampshire in 1789 (DeVault & Weaver, 1970).

The "Rules, Memorize, and Practice" Script

The first American mathematics textbook to address the growing need for arithmetic instruction was Nicolas Pike's *Arithmetic*, published in 1788. The teaching process in Pike's book was as follows: state a rule, give an example, and have students complete a set of practice exercises (Jones & Coxford, 1970). It is critical to note that this was the first mathematics instructional approach in the United States. This approach established a script for mathematics teaching and learning that became deeply embedded in our culture and expected by students and parents alike.

As a result of this initial and enduring teaching script, nearly every adult has the same idea of what a mathematics teacher is supposed to do: state a rule, demonstrate a solution procedure with examples, and then have students practice problems just like the demonstrated examples. It is highly likely that this is the instructional approach you experienced as a student yourself, and the approach your parents experienced and their parents before them (Hiebert, 2013).

Reflections for **Parents**

Did you experience the "rules, memorize, and practice" script when you were a mathematics student? If so, how did it shape your learning of mathematics? Do you remember a time in grade school, middle school, or high school when mathematics became hard to learn using that script?

Because this mathematics teaching script is so embedded in our culture, whenever administrators or other school leaders try to change the script, students, parents, community members, and even some educators frequently oppose these change efforts. As Patricia Cohen (2003) eloquently states, "Americans live in the shadow, still, of the ideas and stereotypes about arithmetic first articulated in the nineteenth century" (p. 70). Some scholars argue that this "shadow" stretches as far back as 14th century Europe when mercantile schools taught commercial arithmetic out of a growing economic need for efficient calculation (Harouni, 2015).

The "Reasoning and Understanding" Script

The first effort to change the mathematics teaching script was Warren Colburn's *An Arithmetic on the Plan of Pestalozzi*, published in 1821. Colburn followed his initial text with a series of updates known under the title *Colburn's First Lessons: Intellectual Arithmetic, Upon the Inductive Method of Instruction* (1826). Colburn offered a different instructional approach. Influenced by the Swiss educator Johann Heinrich Pestalozzi, Colburn's approach used a series of carefully sequenced questions and concrete materials so students could discover mathematical rules for themselves. Colburn's text "proposed problems that were to be reasoned out, often orally, rather than solved by direct application of rules" (Jones & Coxford, 1970, p. 26). Colburn went so far as to argue that teachers postpone practice until after students develop understanding (DeVault & Weaver, 1970). However, Colburn also emphasized that students must learn mental arithmetic (Cohen, 2003).

Should teachers offer students rules and facts to memorize? Or should they give students material to reason about in order to discover and develop understanding of underlying mathematical principles?

By the 1830s, there was already backlash to Colburn's reasoning and understanding approach. A text published in Philadelphia, *The Southern and Western Calculator* (Bridge, 1831), declares "that rules were necessary and pupils could not be expected to invent them" (Cohen, 2003, p. 62). Bates Botham's text *The Common School Arithmetic* (published in 1832) proudly proclaims that "it would satisfy parents who longed for arithmetic taught 'the good old fashioned way'" (Cohen, 2003, p. 62) with concise and plain explanations of rules.

From the 1820s through the 1850s, those involved in teaching mathematics debated whether a focus on reasoning and understanding or rote learning was most appropriate (Cohen, 2003). So within the first half century of the founding of the United States, the great mathematics debate was established. Should teachers offer students rules and facts to memorize? Or should they give students material to reason about in order to discover and develop understanding of underlying mathematical principles?

Reflections for **Parents**

Did you experience the "reasoning and understanding" script when you were a mathematics student? If so, how did it shape your learning of mathematics? Do you remember a time in grade school, middle school, or high school when mathematics became hard to learn using that script?

First Half of the 20th Century: The Cycle Repeats

Colburn's approach was never seriously implemented, and the publication of Thorndike's (1922) *The Psychology of Arithmetic* cemented traditional instructional approaches in the psyche of the United States. Thorndike emphasized the establishment of mental bonds through extensive practice. But Thorndike's approach also resulted in a fragmentation of the content into many small facts and skills. Students were supposed to learn, memorize, and be tested on these isolated skills and procedures separately, with little regard to understanding (Jones & Coxford, 1970). This meant that students must learn one hundred addition facts with little to no stress on principles such as *commutativity* (adding numbers in any order), which would have reduced by half the number of facts to be memorized. For example, if you know that five plus six equals eleven, and you can add in any order (the commutative property of addition), then you also know that six plus five equals eleven. Five plus six and six plus five become one addition fact, and there is no need to memorize them as two separate facts. The same property works for multiplication (but not for subtraction or division).

Once again, efforts to swing the pendulum emerged. In the late 1930s, William Brownell introduced the meaning theory of learning. According to Brownell (1935), the

> ultimate purpose of arithmetic instruction is the development of the ability to *think* in quantitative situations. The word "think" is used advisedly: the ability merely to perform certain operations mechanically and automatically is not enough. Children must be able to analyze real or described quantitative situations. (p. 28)

Brownell's meaning theory coincided with emerging concerns that became evident in World War II: American recruits did not have sufficient mathematical skills (for example, basic computational and problem-solving skills). Supported with funding from the newly formed National Science Foundation, the 1950s saw the formation of several working groups focused on developing secondary mathematics programs to improve mathematics teaching and learning. These programs collectively became known as *new math*, and the working groups developed curriculum that emphasized the structure of mathematics and coherent explanations for the procedures taught in schools.

New Math: The 1950s and 1960s

Mathematicians led the new math era to bring school mathematics more in line with the mathematics taught at the university level (Kilpatrick, 2014). To a certain extent, mathematicians were also reacting to outcomes of the progressive era of education (1920–1950), which emphasized practical applications of mathematics over the study of the discipline itself, and the perception (real or not) that academic expectations for learning mathematics had been lowered (Klein, 2003).

The proponents of new math generally believed that traditional mathematics instruction relied too heavily on memorization, and they sought to emphasize the underlying structure of mathematics and conceptual understanding.

The period from new math (the late 1950s) to 1980 has been described as a cycle of "crisis-reform-reaction episodes" (Fey & Graeber, 2003, p. 521). The first crisis was a result of concerns that became evident in World War II. In addition, the Soviet launching of *Sputnik* in 1957 drew attention to shortcomings in American mathematics and science education. These conditions created an environment favorable to the reform of mathematics education. The proponents of new math generally believed that traditional mathematics instruction relied too heavily on memorization, and they sought to emphasize the underlying structure of mathematics and conceptual understanding rather than the learning of isolated skills and facts.

The proponents of new math also advocated for a shift in instruction to discovery teaching approaches versus rote learning, and they wanted students to understand the structure of mathematics, how mathematical ideas fit together, and the reasoning methods of pure mathematics. They also wanted to help students develop the habits of mind of mathematicians (Fey & Graeber, 2003). And in language that could have been borrowed from Colburn more than one hundred years earlier, the proponents of new math argued that instruction should "first introduce key concepts and skills as the 'necessary foundation' for the 'related development' of 'appropriate skills' and the 'ability to use mathematics effectively'" (Phillips, 2015, p. 82).

Backlash to New Math: The 1970s

As Phillips (2015) states, "Anyone who knows anything about the new math knows that it failed" (p. 121). New math was essentially over by the early 1970s. Some of the criticisms of the new math era are very similar to criticisms of the CCSS for mathematics. These concerns included the belief that new math constituted a national curriculum, usurped state and local control, and challenged teachers' voices in education (Phillips, 2015).

A 1972 article in the *Washington Post* spoke to the frustration of many parents of elementary students in new math programs (Mathews, 1972). In the article, James Shackelford describes the difficulties he had with new math when he tried to help his daughter with homework from her elementary mathematics book. Shackelford argues that as a chemist, he should be able to understand his daughter's elementary mathematics homework. However, he couldn't because new math was overly and unnecessarily complicated. As we will see in the next chapter, Shackelford's concerns were very similar to the concerns of some parents when facing the Common Core.

It was a widely held belief that new math failed because it did not raise computation scores. However, research on the effectiveness of new math generally shows only small differences between student achievement in traditional and new math programs (Fey & Graeber, 2003). And although raising computation scores was never the goal of new math developers, this belief was popularized in books like Morris Kline's (1973) *Why Johnny Can't Add*. You may or may not recall, but the public perception was that new math was a failure and the movement was doomed.

Research on the effectiveness of new math generally shows only small differences between student achievement in traditional and new math programs.

It is worth noting that Phillips (2015), in his history of new math, argues that new math didn't necessarily have to fail. He offers the idea that the proponents of new math could have taken a different path. They

> could have focused on making sure students simply "understood" the mechanisms behind the traditional algorithms, thereby making them "meaningful." Instead, they focused on introducing an entirely new way of conceptualizing arithmetic, based on a claim about the underlying structure of mathematical knowledge. (pp. 90–91)

In other words, the proponents of new math failed because they swung the mathematics education pendulum too far in one direction.

Back to the Basics: The 1970s and 1980s

If new math had simply attached understanding to skill mastery, perhaps the cyclical swing in mathematics education would have ended in the 1960s. Perhaps your personal experience as a mathematics student in school would have been different. But new math ultimately overemphasized the underlying structure of mathematics, and some of the elementary programs of the era were indeed overly formal and decreased the instructional emphasis on computation (Klein, 2003).

In a reaction opposite to the new math era, the 1970s and 1980s became known as a "back to the basics" period (Fey & Graeber, 2003). The back to the basics movement emphasized procedural arithmetic skills, clearly defined behavioral learning objectives, direct instruction aimed at student mastery of the objectives, and the extensive use of local and national standardized tests to measure student attainment of mostly low-level, skill-oriented objectives (Fey & Graeber, 2003). The back to the basics movement affected mathematics instruction but also, to some extent, was part of the general societal reaction to the 1960s.

Origin of Standards-Based Mathematics Education Reform: The 1980s

By the 1980s, people were raising concerns that students were not learning enough mathematics. NCTM, founded in 1920, is the world's largest mathematics education organization and is considered the public voice and foremost authority in mathematics education. Based on a series of reports, surveys, and conferences conducted in the 1970s, NCTM's efforts to improve mathematics education culminated in the document *An Agenda for Action* (NCTM, 1980). This document recommended that problem solving become the focus of school mathematics, and that basic skills should be defined more broadly than simple arithmetic (Fey & Graeber, 2003).

> *By the 1980s, people were raising concerns that students were not learning enough mathematics.*

Another crisis created an environment that would make it possible to once again reform mathematics education. The highly critical report on American education, *A Nation at Risk* (National Commission on Excellence in Education [NCEE], 1983) states that "if an unfriendly foreign power had attempted to impose on America the mediocre educational performance that exists today, we might well have viewed it as an act of war" (p. 5). It is worth noting that the report went so far as to argue that America had "squandered the gains in student achievement made in the wake of the *Sputnik* challenge" (NCEE, 1983, p. 5).

These events further encouraged NCTM to work to define the mathematics content knowledge all students should be able to know and learn, creating an environment in which people would once again support education reform and recommendations (McLeod, 2003). Eventually, this led to the publication of *Curriculum and Evaluation Standards for School Mathematics* (NCTM, 1989). According to Kilpatrick (2014), the original document was unique in several ways, including:

- The NCTM standards were the product of a professional teachers' organization and not a government agency. They were also the first set of national curricular standards created in any K–12 subject area. This is significant because the tradition of local control of K–12 education made the concept of national standards a controversial endeavor, even if they were voluntary and created by a professional organization (McLeod, 2003).

- The NCTM standards initially received no outside funding. According to Douglas McLeod (2003), this is significant because the NCTM standards had a degree of independence that other curriculum areas did not have. Standards in other curriculum areas created after the NCTM standards received federal funding and, consequently, had to follow federal guidelines.

♦ The NCTM standards were the first effort to go beyond local and state boundaries to put forth national recommendations for the mathematics learning of all students.

While never the original intent of NCTM, the 1989 publication of Curriculum and Evaluation Standards for School Mathematics *(NCTM, 1989) gave birth to the standards-based education reform effort.*

The 1989 NCTM document outlined general mathematics content standards for K–4, 5–8, and 9–12 grade bands. It intentionally did not specify content by grade level, electing to leave that decision to states and local school districts. NCTM followed up the 1989 curriculum standards with *Professional Standards for Teaching Mathematics* (NCTM, 1991), *Assessment Standards for School Mathematics* (NCTM, 1995), and *Principles and Standards for School Mathematics* (NCTM, 2000), which updated and, to some extent, combined the original three standards documents into one document.

While never the original intent of NCTM, the 1989 publication of *Curriculum and Evaluation Standards for School Mathematics* (NCTM, 1989) gave birth to the standards-based education reform effort that characterized the next three decades of mathematics education in the United States—and still dominates 21st century improvement efforts.

Backlash to the Standards: The 1990s and 2000s

By the mid-1990s, forty-one states had created state mathematics standards or curriculum frameworks consistent with NCTM standards (McLeod, 2003). The NCTM standards also served as a model for other subjects, as professional organizations in science, social studies, language arts, physical education, and art worked during the 1990s to develop standards in their disciplines.

However, by the late 1990s, parents and many others began to criticize the NCTM standards, which had started out with a great deal of consensus and broad support (forty professional organizations endorsed or supported the original standards). The backlash was most virulent in California, where the math wars of the late 1990s and early part of the next century originated. Groups such as Mathematically Correct sprang up for those who opposed the NCTM standards or the curriculum that they inspired.

Most of the concerns were familiar: the new standards did not suf-
ficiently emphasize procedural skills, they decreased the emphasis on
repeated practice and memorization, and they provided insufficient
emphasis on direct instruction. In addition, some mathematicians raised
concerns that certain topics (proof and traditional algorithms) were
neglected in the standards, while others received too much emphasis
(probability and data analysis) (McLeod, 2003).

People typically interpret their state standards through
the curriculum implemented in their children's schools.
But the curriculum is not always consistent with what
the authors of NCTM's standards envisioned. Mis-
interpretations of the 1989 standards abounded. The
standards included tables with topics and approaches for
increased or decreased instructional attention. In some
cases, publishers misinterpreted *decrease*, and schools
implemented at the school level as *eliminate*. But the central issue with
the NCTM standards was the enduring historical problem of mathematics education in the United States. "Parents expected teachers to
fulfill the traditional role of transmitter of knowledge to students, but
reformers asked teachers to encourage students to do their own thinking" (McLeod, 2003, p. 808).

> *People typically
> interpret their state
> standards through
> the curriculum
> implemented in their
> children's schools.*

By 2010, the math wars had largely subsided. The publication of
Adding It Up by the NRC in 2001 (see chapter 4) sought to find common ground on both sides of America's traditional great mathematics
education debate (Kilpatrick, Swafford, & Findell, 2001). Could a focus
on skills and procedures coexist with an emphasis on problem solving
and reasoning? Could students experience both types of mathematics
content and demonstrate learning accordingly?

In chapter 4 of this book, we will demonstrate that the answer has
to be *yes*. Unfortunately, the passage of NCLB in 2001 usurped the
equilibrium solution first offered in *Adding It Up*. In 2006, President
George W. Bush formed the National Mathematics Advisory Panel
(NMAP) and modeled it after the National Reading Panel that preceded
it. One of the goals of the National Reading Panel was to end the reading wars. To some extent, the debate in mathematics education in the
1990s mirrored the whole language versus phonics debate in reading.

Opponents to NCTM's standards often borrowed language from the reading wars. In Presidential Executive Order 13398 in 2006, President Bush charged NMAP with reviewing and summarizing the scientific evidence related to mathematics teaching and learning (NMAP, 2008).

NMAP's (2008) final report finds that "all-encompassing recommendations that instruction should be entirely 'student centered' or 'teacher directed' are not supported by research" (p. xxii). In addition, the panel concludes that the "curriculum must simultaneously develop conceptual understanding, computational fluency, and problem-solving skills. Debates regarding the relative importance of these aspects of mathematical knowledge are misguided" (NMAP, 2008, p. xix).

However, NCLB usurped this attempt to offer an equilibrium path forward for mathematics education.

The panel's report is often credited with ending the math wars, but a third event was perhaps more significant. The passage of the NCLB fundamentally changed the focus of mathematics instruction at the local school level. NCLB required states to annually test students in grades 3 through 8 and in one grade in high school. Mathematics curriculum and instruction were increasingly narrowed to focus on the content to be assessed on state tests. Once again, it became the norm to provide direct instruction on those skills, National Science Foundation curricula fell out of favor, and the math wars faded into the past as the battles over new math had faded forty years earlier. Teachers, administrators, and school districts now emphasized the need to produce good test scores on assessments that unfortunately, once again, primarily defined mathematics as procedural skills knowledge with low-level application.

Eventually, however, the flaws and unintended consequences of NCLB became clear to more educators as well as politicians. The Every Student Succeeds Act (ESSA) (P.L. 114-95) replaced NCLB in December 2015 to take effect in the 2016–2017 school year. ESSA retains annual testing in grades 3–8 and once in high school, but it allows states flexibility in how and when they administer tests and offers a broader mix of factors in state accountability systems (for example, accountability systems could include measures of teacher engagement) (Klein, 2015).

As described in the introduction and chapter 1 of this book (pages 1 and 9), the incoherent NCLB system of fifty different sets of standards, tests, and passing scores—as well as demonstrated overstatements of student proficiency when state test results were compared to NAEP results (Achieve, 2015)—led the National Governors Association to propose the development of what became known as the CCSS for mathematics.

Lessons to Learn

Although brief and oversimplified, we have documented the history of mathematics education in the United States as a two hundred–year pendulum swing between an overemphasis on the rote practice of isolated skills and procedures, and an overemphasis on conceptual understanding, with their respective overreliance on either teacher-directed or student-centered instruction.

Reflections for **Parents**

Reflect once again on your own mathematics learning as you were growing up. This most likely affects your beliefs concerning mathematics education in general. If you learned mathematics in the 1970s or 1980s, chances are you were part of the back-to-basics and rote memorized drill movement. If you learned mathematics in the 1990s, you were entering the problem-solving and reasoning era.

You probably became aware that the pendulum had swung if the mathematics curriculum and instruction your child experienced in school looked dramatically different from your own. Based on information in chapter 1, it should be clear that when the mathematics curriculum and instruction pendulum swings too far in either direction, students are generally not well served.

When a pendulum is at rest in its equilibrium position, it is halfway between the two poles. We believe the equilibrium position, which balances the emphasis on procedures and conceptual understanding, is the best way forward for mathematics education. In chapter 3, we help you understand the actual intent of the CCSS initiative by examining the debate over the CCSS that emerged in earnest during 2014–2015 and the residual effects of that debate for mathematics education moving forward.

Questions for Reflection

Reflecting on your reading is an opportunity to evaluate and deepen your understanding, gain additional insight, and apply what you have read to your own specific context (Costa & Kallick, 2008). Whether you are an educator or parent, we encourage you to use these questions for personal reflection or to prompt discussion with colleagues and friends if you are reading the book together with the goal of understanding and improving mathematics learning in your local schools.

Questions for Educators

1. What period reflects your own personal mathematics learning experience? Does it match the description offered here?

2. What did you like or dislike about learning mathematics during that period? What would have helped you learn mathematics more effectively?

3. How does the way you learned mathematics affect how you teach mathematics? Or, if you are a school leader, how does it influence what you expect to see in the classroom?

Questions for Parents

1. How much of the mathematical rules, procedures, and definitions you learned and memorized in school do you remember? Does it reflect the way you use mathematics in your daily life?

2. What period reflects your own personal mathematics learning experience? Does it match the description offered here?

3. What did you like or dislike about learning mathematics when you were in school? What would have helped you learn mathematics more effectively?

Chapter 3

The Common Core Mathematics Debate

An excellent mathematics program includes curriculum that develops important mathematics along coherent learning progressions and develops connections among areas of mathematical study and between mathematics and the real world.

—NCTM

This chapter will help you better understand and speak to the original intent, hope, and promise of the Common Core as well as the arguments against them. As you read through these issues, ask yourself, "How will or does this affect the students in my class or my school, the current high school graduates in my district, or any graduating class moving forward? What is the truth about the expectations of the revised mathematics standards?"

If you are an elementary educator, students' parents might have expressed concern about the nature of homework labeled *Common Core.* This chapter will help you better understand the intent of the Common Core, gain insight into the arguments some parents and politicians make against the Common Core, equip you to discuss those issues and concerns with parents, and help you determine if elementary-level math homework really has anything to do with the actual content standards of the Common Core. (See Issue 3: Challenges of Authentic Implementation, page 50, for more insight.)

Reflections for **Parents**

Some of you may have children born in 2010, or perhaps these children live on your street or in your neighborhood. In all likelihood, they will be the first class of students to receive a K–12 education built on a foundation of mathematics standards influenced by the Common Core—a call for a balanced student learning experience. Is this a good or a bad outcome for your child? Will it better prepare your child (and all of those who come before and after) for college and career readiness after high school? What have your friends and neighbors said about the expectations of the Common Core? This chapter will help you better understand the difference between the Common Core as a set of state designed standards *and* the Common Core as a testing process for those state standards.

Support for the CCSS for Mathematics

It was April 2009 when the Council of Chief State School Officers (CCSSO; composed of State Department of Education leaders) and the National Governors Association Center for Best Practices advocated for and sponsored the development of a common set of mathematics content standards for K–12 students in the United States. They were aiming to improve opportunities for students learning now and in the future.

The goal was to ensure all students leave high school prepared for college and career. Published in June of 2010, these standards became known as the CCSS for mathematics, or simply the Common Core (NGA & CCSSO, 2010). (The NGA and CCSSO also released standards for English language arts at this time.) Visit the Common Core's website (www.corestandards.org) to download and read more about the standards.

Both democrat and republican governors supported the standards. Some governors who opposed the Common Core later originally supported the standards.

The political response to the birth of these K–12 standards was a relatively uncontroversial endeavor and a bipartisan initiative (Supovitz, Daly, & del Fresno, n.d.). Both democrat and republican governors supported the standards. Some governors who opposed the Common Core later originally supported the standards (Kertscher, 2015; Layton, 2015; & Qiu, 2015). Eventually, forty-five states and the District of Columbia adopted the *voluntary* mathematics standards. And states like Alaska, Texas, Minnesota, Nebraska, and Virginia developed their own state standards that reflected some of the best elements of the CCSS for mathematics.

The future looked promising for improving student learning in mathematics not only for those born in 2010 but also for the class of 2015 and beyond. There was great hope and enthusiasm that learning expectations for mathematics would and could be raised and equalized—that students from Mississippi to Massachusetts would learn both more mathematics and essentially the same mathematics.

Why did the states' governors and chief state school leaders feel compelled to commission the writing of these standards? Partially because as the 21st century opened, some politicians and educators became increasingly aware that the patchwork quilt of various state standards, expectations, and tests resulted in vastly different learning outcomes for students (see chapter 1). The quality of education wasn't just about being born in 2010. It was more about the zip code in which you were born. This is a harsh reality in the United States. Contrary to the rhetoric, the United States is not a country of equal education outcomes or even opportunities (Schmidt, Cogan, Houang, & McKnight, 2011).

> *The quality of education wasn't just about being born in 2010. It was more about the zip code in which you were born. This is a harsh reality in the United States. Contrary to the rhetoric, the United States is not a country of equal education outcomes or even opportunities.*

Students were learning different amounts of mathematics at different levels of proficiency based on little more than where they lived because each state determined its own standards. How much education a student attains and how much mathematics a student learns in grades K–12 has significant implications for his or her career and economic growth opportunities in society (Autor, 2014; Carnevale et al., 2015; NRC, 2012a). Consequently, this should be a major concern for every parent.

Objections to the CCSS for Mathematics

In 2015, as the high school class of 2028 prepared to enter kindergarten, the same Common Core that enjoyed near universal support from teachers, education leaders, politicians, and even many parents just two years prior were suddenly under assault from a variety of directions. Why? Social historians will eventually analyze what happened and offer various theories.

We briefly point out why we believe some support was lost and illustrate what has never been a serious point of opposition to the CCSS for mathematics: *the content and process standards themselves*—the statements of what students should know and be able to *do* with mathematics. The motivation for opposing the Common Core is different for different individuals and groups.

Issue 1: Mistaken Belief That the Common Core Is a Federal Initiative

The federal government attached Race to the Top funds (see www2 .ed.gov/programs/racetothetop/index.html for additional information) to state adoption of college- and career-ready standards, which led to this mistaken perception. Grant applicants, at either the state or district level, widely interpreted this grant requirement as the federal government's effort to "force" adoption of the CCSS. In reality, all states had to do was adopt college- and career-ready standards. States never were specifically required to adopt the Common Core, although adopting it was perhaps the most efficient way to demonstrate that local standards were college and career ready.

Education in the United States has always been a state, and even more specifically, a local issue. Therefore, some people objected to the Common Core because they saw it as federal intrusion on states' rights, despite the fact that the states' governors and chief state school leaders commissioned the CCSS back in 2009. In reality, the Common Core movement originated at the state level and was directed at the state level—the very states that have constitutional authority for education in the United States.

Some people objected to the Common Core because they saw it as federal intrusion on states' rights, despite the fact that the states' governors and chief state school leaders commissioned the CCSS back in 2009.

Issue 2: Confusion Between Standards and State Testing of Standards

Ever since NCLB passed in 2001, states have been required to annually test students in grades 3 through 8 and in one grade in high school. Federal support of education is not a new phenomenon. The most significant federal legislation affecting education was and remains the ESEA of 1965 (PL 89-10). This legislation sought to narrow achievement gaps by providing resources to support instructional materials and professional development for educators. The federal government intended to reauthorize ESEA every five years, but NCLB remained the version of the ESEA through the 2015–2016 school year. ESEA was reauthorized, beginning with the 2016–2017 school year, as the Every Student Succeeds Act of 2015 (P.L. 114-95).

NCLB supported standards-based reform, assessment, and establishing measurable goals—a requirement that disaggregated groups of students make adequate yearly progress in mathematics and reading. President George W. Bush proposed NCLB, and both democrats and republicans sponsored it. Both houses of Congress passed it overwhelmingly.

Under the guidelines of NCLB, each state was required to develop its own test and its own passing score (definition of proficiency) for grades 3–8 and high school. This resulted in little consistency in expectations across states and an incoherent system of fifty different sets of standards, with fifty different tests of mathematics proficiency, and fifty different passing scores. If a student was declared proficient in mathematics in one state, he or she might or might not be proficient in another state—it was simply impossible to tell (Fuller, Wright, Gesicki, & Kang, 2007).

In 2010, with the wide adoption of the CCSS, many education leaders believed the next logical step was to develop common assessments (with an eye on improvement over the current state assessments) that could be used to determine how well students were acquiring the adopted CCSS.

In 2010, with the wide adoption of the CCSS, many education leaders believed the next logical step was to develop common assessments (with an eye on improvement over the current state assessments).

They intended to develop common tests of mathematics proficiency so student achievement could be compared from state to state. In 2010, the U.S. Department of Education awarded more than $330 million in Race to the Top funds to two consortia, at the time representing the majority of states, to develop assessments aligned with the CCSS that would replace the various state tests. Initially, more than thirty states belonged to one or both of the consortia. However, beginning in 2015, some states began to withdraw from the assessment consortia, and once again began to design their own assessments.

The states that represented the SMARTER Balanced Assessment Consortium (SBAC) received $160 million, and the states that represented the Partnership for Assessment of Readiness for College and Careers (PARCC) received $176 million to design improved tests (Porter, McMaken, Hwang, & Yang, 2011). The first testing occurred in the spring of 2015. As the assessments are being administered and results are announced, what is most likely to happen to the standards and the new assessments by 2020? By 2025?

First, these Common Core state assessments (SBAC, PARCC, or a new state-based assessment) are radically different from the state assessments that preceded them. The design specifications for these tests, and the released sample items, assess students' abilities to engage in higher-order thinking, reasoning and conceptual understanding, and problem solving.

Previously, state assessments under NCLB assessed basic skills in isolation at a low-level depth of knowledge (Herman & Linn, 2013). The new tests are delivered in a modern-day digital medium, which means online with a mix of constructed-response items (students must provide the answer, not choose from multiple-choice answers), performance-based tasks (problems that require extended solutions), and computer-enhanced items that require the application of knowledge and skills. It's important to note that the nature of all testing for college and career readiness pursuits, as well as much of the technical diagnostic work done in schools, is now administered in an online environment.

In most cases, initial implementation of these new forms of student assessment occurred in the spring of 2015, as a growing grassroots movement against testing in general emerged in the United States. This so-called "opt-out" movement includes a very small but vocal group of parents who refuse to allow their children to take the new assessments.

Parents and some education leaders began to express legitimate concerns related to testing, including the following (Larson & Leinwand, 2013c).

- The amount of time devoted to testing in schools at the expense of instruction

- The cost of testing, exacerbated by the infrastructure requirements of online administration of the new tests

- Data collection and privacy concerns related to the use and storage of student results

- The use of assessment results to evaluate teachers, especially when the tests were widely acknowledged to be more rigorous and likely to result in lower test scores

In October 2015, the Obama administration acknowledged the United States' overemphasis on standardized testing and recommended that standardized testing be capped at 2 percent of students' classroom time, while simultaneously reinforcing the point that appropriate assessment is an important instructional tool (Lederman & Kerr, 2015). These recommendations hold the promise to address some of the concerns of the opt-out movement. State and national consortia tests must be continually revised and improved if there is to be effective growth and development in standards assessment. The important point is that efficiency and implementation concerns directed at the *assessment* of the CCSS should not be confused with the value of the K–12 mathematics *content* of the Common Core standards initiative.

The important point is that efficiency and implementation concerns directed at the assessment of the CCSS should not be confused with the value of the K–12 mathematics content of the Common Core standards initiative.

Assessing what a student *has* learned (How will we know if students have mastered the standards?) is a distinct matter and process from what each student *should* learn (What do we want every student to know and be able to do?) in mathematics at each grade level. Every child has the right to be college and career ready when he or she leaves high school.

As we will explain in chapter 4, assessment at the local and state levels is a critical part of an effective K–12 mathematics program. As highly respected U.S. mathematics educators Mark Hoover Thames and Deborah Ball (2013) write: "If the country is to make progress on improving mathematics education, then the all-too-common aversion to assessment among professional educators . . . is untenable. Testing (in some form) is critical to education" (p. 37).

We would add students' families to the list of those who should not be averse to embracing the role assessment plays in improving instruction and student learning.

Reflections for **Parents**

A medical analogy is useful to illustrate the value of assessment to instruction. When a person goes to his or her physician with a medical concern, the first thing the physician typically does is conduct an assessment, which often includes ordering a test (for example, a blood test, an X-ray, or perhaps a CT scan) in order to diagnose the problem and determine the most effective treatment. Assessment in education diagnoses student learning needs and directs effective instruction to respond to those needs just as medical tests diagnose illness and direct effective treatment protocols. Opting out of assessment that reflects student learning is the equivalent of opting out of potentially life-saving medical tests.

Issue 3: Challenges of Authentic Implementation

Teaching the revised mathematics standards requires professional development and support to make the transition to these new, more rigorous standards. As a result, some teachers are still in the process of learning how to interpret the content standards; use research-affirmed, highly effective instructional strategies (see chapter 4); and increase their own mathematical knowledge for teaching more rigorous content standards. In an era of viral social media reactions (see issue 4, page 52), parents and many others began to circulate and decry what they saw as confusing and needlessly complicated instruction and homework.

A fairly famous example of frustrating homework mistakenly credited to the Common Core standards came from parent Jeff Severt (Heitin, 2014). In early spring 2014, Severt posted a page from his second-grade son's Common Core homework on Facebook. The assignment required his son to determine where a fictional student named Jack went wrong when computing 427 minus 316.

Severt, who has a bachelor's degree in engineering, completed his son's homework using the traditional algorithm in under five seconds. He objected to Jack's approach of using a number line and skip-counting backward to solve the equation—an overly complex approach to the problem, from his perspective. The assignment asked students to write a letter to Jack explaining what he should do to fix his mistake. Severt completed his son's letter to Jack, telling Jack that he shouldn't feel bad about his mistake because he himself has a degree in electronics engineering, has completed extensive college-level mathematics courses, and that despite his mathematical background, even he couldn't explain Common Core mathematics. This concern is nearly identical to that Shackelford expressed half a century earlier with respect to new math (see chapter 2, page 27). Severt signed the letter *Frustrated Parent*. His Facebook post went viral, and conservative talk show host Glenn Beck interviewed him on his television program (Atler, 2014).

Bill McCallum, one of the lead writers commissioned by the states' governors for the development of the CCSS for mathematics, reported that the problem was not a Common Core problem but a product of poorly designed curriculum. The Common Core actually requires fluency in the skills of adding and subtracting using the same strategy Severt used to solve the problem (Garland, 2014).

However, some parents reached the conclusion that what they perceived as senseless and unnecessarily convoluted instruction and homework was a result of Common Core implementation. The often repeated mantra was, "If we hadn't adopted the Common Core, we wouldn't have to suffer from this confusing and senseless homework." Is this something you have heard as well? Have you heard people equate "confusing instruction" and "confusing homework" with "Common Core instruction and homework"? This could not be further from the truth.

It is worth noting that the writers of the CCSS for mathematics (and English language arts) specifically state, "These standards do not dictate curriculum or teaching methods" (NGA & CCSSO, 2010, p. 5). Unfortunately, this critical yet very subtle statement from the CCSS initiative document never went viral.

Nearly all the instructional and homework tasks or examples that rightly frustrate parents are not examples of what is necessary for every student to know and be able to do at each grade level or course (in other words, these examples do not exemplify the CCSS initiative). Instead, they are often examples, tasks, or methods of ineffective instruction; they represent a poor interpretation of the curriculum and the standards; or they represent instructional strategies used to develop student understanding of underlying mathematical concepts. However, they aren't the end goal of instruction. It is critical not to confuse instructional strategies intended to build understanding with end goals that include proficiency with standard or traditional approaches. (We describe effective instruction in chapter 4.)

In general, when frustration sets in for students, parents, or teachers, there is a tendency to want to place blame and find a scapegoat. The Common Core became a bogeyman for every concern anyone had about mathematics education. With respect to most of these concerns, the bogeyman existed prior to 2010, but now he had a new, high-profile identity.

How can we claim in the United States—which prides itself on equality of opportunity—that a college- and career-ready K–12 curriculum is not for every student?

All too often, the reaction to this criticism is to lower the bar of expectations. It would be easier in some ways not to expect too much of our students, our educators, and ourselves. Yet, how can we choose to lower the bar for what every student should know and be able to do? How can we claim in the United States—which prides itself on equality of opportunity—that a college- and career-ready K–12 curriculum is not for every student?

Implementation frustrations aside, the CCSS, if effectively interpreted and implemented, are a source of great promise and hope—not something to blame for every frustration someone has regarding school.

Issue 4: Social Media—Opinion Versus Evidence

The news media, in general, does not often cite research or rely on experts when offering stories on education (Henig, 2008). And yet, the news media can and does significantly influence people's perceptions of issues (Yettick, 2015). Social media has amplified this effect. The

Internet has changed our lives. It is now possible to do our own research and ultimately become "experts" ourselves. However, we must keep this caution in the back of our minds (Pariser, 2011). As an article in *National Geographic* points out, the "Internet has democratized information, which is a good thing. But along with cable TV, it has made it possible to live in a 'filter bubble' that lets in only the information with which you already agree" (Achenbach, 2015, p. 45).

People who have concerns about the Common Core or the testing of those standards, based on their own experiences, can quickly find an entire social network of like-minded individuals with whom they could share examples of ineffective instruction and curriculum and virally spread misinformation within an increasingly loud echo chamber (Castillo, Mendoza, & Poblete, 2011; Roodhouse, 2009). The same could be said for those who support the standards.

Social networks, such as Facebook and Twitter, often fan the fires of the debate over the Common Core and give voice to grassroots critics in unprecedented ways. Jonathan Supovitz, Alan Daly, and Miguel del Fresno's (n.d.) extensive study on the impact of social media on the Common Core debate analyzes nearly 190,000 tweets made between September 2013 and March 2014 using the hashtag #commoncore. Their research is fascinating. We highlight some of their findings here.

- The elite transmitters (the individuals who sent out the most tweets) are overwhelmingly against the Common Core (by a margin of more than four to one).

- The most frequently mentioned education topic with the hashtag #commoncore is *testing*. (See issue 2 on page 46.)

- Those supporting the Common Core tend to form their arguments using logical reasoning and facts.

- Those who opposed the Common Core tend to use more visceral language, appeal to people's passions, and utilize powerful metaphors. See, for example, "Common Core as a Threat to Freedom" (Supovitz et al., n.d., p. 53) and "Common Core as a Source of Psychological Harm" (Supovitz et al., n.d., p. 52).

Social media is a powerful force in generating and inflaming opposition to the CCSS initiative, while reinforcing the misinformation outlined in issues 1 through 3.

Reflections for **Parents**

We recommend trying to ignore anyone speaking in extremes about the mathematics your child is learning, not offering constructive suggestions for improvement, or not providing evidence to support his or her claims. Challenge your friends and colleagues to actually read the CCSS for mathematics (www.corestandards.org). We encourage you to consult the literature we cite if you want more information. Seek to understand the CCSS for mathematics from an informed point of view based on evidence and not simply someone's opinion—an opinion that may or may not be steeped in the actual facts and evidence. We encourage you to understand issues based on the evidence, and leave the rhetoric to talk show hosts. As Douglas Reeves (2011) points out, "Discussions in education often remain stubbornly focused on experience instead of evidence. . . . Rhetorical certitude, however, is not a substitute for evidence" (p. 5).

What Few Seem to Oppose: Good Standards

We offer these four issues for objection to the CCSS in order to shine a bright light on the following: *Not one of the four issues has anything to do with the K–12 mathematics content of the state standards themselves.*

For example, no one seriously argues that the third-grade treatment of fractions in the Common Core is misguided or that the developmental progression of fractions in grades 3–5 is inappropriate. There is actually very strong agreement on *what we want every student to know and be able to do* (Munter, Stein, & Smith, 2015), but too often that is masked behind a smoke screen of unrelated issues and concerns.

In a fascinating paradox, the CCSS for mathematics often calls for student learning that is the exact opposite of what is attributed to the initiative (for mathematics) and posted on social media. Contrary to what often appears on Facebook and Twitter, the Common Core *does* call for students to learn how to add, subtract, multiply, and divide with whole numbers, integers (positive and negative numbers with no fractional part), and rationals (fractions), and to ultimately do so with traditional algorithms—the way you learned it when you were in school!

Consider an example from the CCSS for mathematics for fifth grade, standard NBT.5: "Fluently multiply multidigit whole numbers using the standard algorithm" (NGA & CCSSO, 2010). Multiply with the *standard algorithm*! Are you surprised? Figure 3.1 illustrates the traditional algorithm for multiplication you likely learned when you were in school.

$$\begin{array}{r} \overset{2}{43} \\ \times\ 17 \\ \hline 301 \\ +\ 430 \\ \hline 731 \end{array}$$

Figure 3.1: Traditional algorithm for multiplication.

While reasonable experts might and do debate the placement of specific topics in certain grade levels in the Common Core, the majority of serious scholarly reviews (a greater level of confidence than just our opinions) find that the CCSS for mathematics are more rigorous, focused, and coherent than the vast majority of state standards that preceded them (Porter et al., 2011; Schmidt & Houang, 2012).

The hope and the promise of the mathematics standards is that those students will graduate from high school better prepared for a post–high school world that demands greater levels of reasoning and understanding than ever before. The hope is that they will demonstrate exceptional procedural fluency, conceptual understanding, and problem-solving ability, and graduate college and career ready with unprecedented opportunities open to them. It appears that is exactly what is happening.

According to Paul Peterson, Samuel Barrows, and Thomas Gift (2016), the CCSS have served as a catalyst to significantly improve student proficiency in mathematics and reading. They claim, "Most states set only mediocre standards for the first 10 years of NCLB. Since 2011, 45 states have raised their standards for proficiency in reading and math based on comparing state and NAEP expectations. The greatest gains occurred between 2013 and 2015" (p. 2).

In their summer 2015 *Education Next* report "States Raise Proficiency Standards in Math and Reading," Paul Peterson and Matthew Ackerman write that twenty-four of forty-nine states earned an A grade for raising the bar of expected proficiencies for every grade level. To read the full report, go to http://educationnext.org/after-common-core-states-set-rigorous-standards/, and see the grade your state received.

In the next chapter, our focus turns to parents and their role in their children's mathematics education. We will more fully define what constitutes an equilibrium position in mathematics education and answer the question, What should students' learning experiences in mathematics look like in the classroom (and at home)?

Questions for Reflection

Reflecting on your reading is an opportunity to evaluate and deepen your understanding, gain additional insight, and apply what you have read to your own specific context (Costa & Kallick, 2008). Whether you are an educator or parent, we encourage you to use these questions for personal reflection or to prompt discussion with colleagues and friends if you are reading the book together with the goal of understanding and improving mathematics learning in your local schools.

Questions for Educators

1. What arguments have you heard people use to criticize the CCSS for mathematics? How have you responded to that criticism? Do you still have unanswered questions from this chapter? What are they?

2. How are criticisms of the CCSS for mathematics similar or dissimilar from previous mathematics education eras, for example, the new math era or the back-to-basics movement?

3. Do you agree with any of the concerns raised about the CCSS for mathematics? Why? How could those concerns be addressed in your current work setting?

Questions for Parents

1. Are you surprised that the Common Core is not a federal initiative? Have you ever confused concerns about testing of the state standards with the actual CCSS themselves?

2. Do you think it makes sense that students' mathematics education in different states is based on different mathematics standards? Or, do you think it is positive that the differences between state standards are narrowing?

3. Do you think it makes sense that states have different expectations and definitions of proficiency for students? Why or why not?

PART II

In part II of this book, the primary audience shifts from educators to parents. The following two chapters define mathematical literacy, highlight elements of mathematics programs that are in a state of equilibrium or balance, and describe essential features of effective mathematics instruction—the instructional strategies parents should expect their children's classroom teachers to employ. Part II also offers suggestions for how parents can help their children learn mathematics at home and at school.

However, educators also can gain much from reading and reflecting on these pages. They will find many feature boxes titled "Reflections for Educators," which offer information they can use to deepen their understanding of mathematical literacy; gain additional insight into effective mathematics instruction; learn how to more effectively communicate with parents about issues regarding mathematics instruction; and identify strategies parents can use to support their children's mathematics learning at home.

Chapter 4

The Equilibrium Position and Effective Mathematics Instruction

Let us teach our children mathematics the honest way by teaching both skills and understanding.

—HUNG-HSI WU,
PROFESSOR EMERITUS OF MATHEMATICS,
UNIVERSITY OF CALIFORNIA, BERKELEY

In a 2012 NRC report, *Education for Life and Work: Developing Transferable Knowledge and Skills in the 21st Century*, the expert panel argues that the competencies necessary to be successful in the 21st century require deeper learning by students—a "process through which an individual becomes capable of taking what was learned in one situation and applying it to new situations (i.e., transfer)" (NRC, 2012a, p. 5). The panel points out that transferable knowledge by students is the product of deeper learning and includes

> content knowledge in a domain and knowledge of how, why, and when to apply this knowledge to answer questions and solve problems. . . . [The needed competencies] are structured around fundamental principles of the content area and their relationships rather than disparate, superficial facts or procedures. (NRC, 2012a, p. 6)

The panel further cites research indicating deeper student learning ultimately produces retention and the ability to transfer knowledge learned at higher performance rates than does rote learning. "Rote learning of solutions to specific problems or problem-solving procedures" will not produce the competencies required in the 21st century (NRC, 2012a, p. 9).

Mathematical Literacy and the Equilibrium Position

A modern definition of *mathematical literacy* includes student development of skills and procedures, conceptual understanding, problem solving, and a disposition to expend effort and persevere when learning mathematics and solving problems. Similarly, the NRC (Kilpatrick et al., 2001, p. 5) defines *mathematical proficiency* as consisting of five interwoven strands.

1. **Procedural fluency** is the skill necessary to carry out procedures flexibly, accurately, efficiently, and appropriately. In elementary school, this would include the ability to carry out routine computations. In secondary school, it would include symbolic manipulations in algebra.

2. **Conceptual understanding** is the comprehension of mathematical concepts, operations, and relations. This focuses on the central and underlying ideas of mathematics and their connections—understanding why a procedure works.

3. **Strategic competence** is the ability to formulate, represent, and solve mathematical problems. This focuses on how to set up problems.

4. **Adaptive reasoning** is the capacity for logical thought, reflection, explanation, and justification. This is the type of reasoning in which mathematicians engage as they create mathematical knowledge.

5. **Productive disposition** is the habitual inclination to see mathematics as sensible, useful, and worthwhile, coupled with a belief in diligence and one's own efficacy. This is sometimes referred to as having a *growth mindset* (Dweck, 2006). For example, do you believe that mathematics is something that you can learn and improve through hard work? A critical component of productive disposition is the development of a robust mathematical identity and sense of agency in each and every student (Aguirre et al., 2013; Leonard, Brooks, Barnes-Johnson, & Berry, 2010).

Perhaps the most important point the authors of the NRC report make about the definition of mathematical proficiency (literacy) is that the five strands "are interwoven and interdependent" (Kilpatrick et al., 2001, p. 5), meaning they support one another. The strands are not separate, a point particularly important with respect to conceptual understanding and procedural fluency (Kilpatrick et al., 2001).

> Procedural fluency and conceptual understanding are often seen as competing for attention in school mathematics. But pitting skill against understanding creates a false dichotomy. . . . Understanding makes learning skills easier, less susceptible to common errors, and less prone to forgetting. By the same token, a certain level of skill is required to learn many mathematical concepts with understanding, and using procedures can help strengthen and develop that understanding. (p. 122)

Reflections for Educators

Mathematics instruction should focus on developing skills *and* understanding for each student, as well as the ability to reason with his or her skills and understanding to solve problems. Skills and understanding clearly support one another, and both are necessary to be an effective problem solver.

Students across grades K–12 need to learn how, why, and when to apply their mathematical skills and conceptual understanding. As this chapter's opening quote by University of California, Berkeley mathematician Hung-Hsi Wu (1999) states, your child needs to acquire both skills *and* understanding—this is the "honest way" forward.

This honest way of learning mathematics is most effectively accomplished when the instructional approach is similarly in equilibrium. In 2005, a group of mathematics educators and mathematicians met to find common ground regarding some of the intractable issues in mathematics education (Ball et al.).

> Students can learn effectively via a mixture of direct instruction, structured investigation, and open exploration. Decisions about what is better taught through direct instruction and what might be better taught by structuring explorations for

,ents should be made on the basis of the particular math-
,atics, the goals for learning, and the students' present skills
ιd knowledge. (p. 1058)

When the mathematics program in your local school is in equilibrium, these traditional opposing forces (skills versus understanding and direct instruction versus discovery) are at rest, *balanced*, and interwoven, and they support one another. Establishing and maintaining equilibrium is an expected part of a highly effective mathematics program.

Effective Mathematics Teaching and Learning

Students' mathematics learning experiences across the United States too often consist of instructional methods you likely experienced as a student: instruction focuses on low-level tasks and emphasizes procedures and memorization. It offers little attention to reasoning, problem solving, and the development of meaning (NRC, 2012a). In these classrooms, you mostly will watch or observe the teacher doing mathematics. But you rarely will see the expected balance of the teacher and your child *doing* the mathematics with peers and with each other.

The NRC (2012a) suggests it is plausible that low levels of student performance in mathematics are a result of this older, more traditional, nonbalanced instructional approach in the United States. U.S. mathematics instruction is finally changing to give students opportunities to learn mathematics with understanding by actively doing mathematics in class (not just watching the teacher do the math) and connecting that work to meaningful tasks related to each standard.

The instructional recommendations in both *Education for Life and Work: Developing Transferable Knowledge and Skills in the 21st Century* (NRC, 2012a) and *Principles to Actions: Ensuring Mathematical Success for All* (NCTM, 2014) provide a consensus about mathematics instruction. These national recommendations include developing the understanding of mathematics skills your child must master as well as his or her ability to reason with those skills and apply understanding to solve problems.

Reflections for Educators

The NRC offers six research-based instructional recommendations to help you promote students' deeper learning (NRC, 2012a). These are consistent with the instructional practices in NCTM's (2014) *Principles to Actions: Ensuring Mathematical Success for All.*

1. **Use multiple and varied representations of concepts and tasks**, such as diagrams, numerical and mathematical representations, and simulations, combined with activities and guidance that support mapping across the varied representations.

2. **Encourage elaboration, questioning, and explanation**; for example, prompt students who are reading a history text to think about the author's intent or to explain specific information and arguments as they read—either silently to themselves or to others.

3. **Engage learners in challenging tasks**, while also supporting them with guidance, feedback, and encouragement to reflect on their own learning process and the status of their understanding.

4. **Teach with examples and cases**, such as modeling step by step how students can carry out a procedure to solve a problem and using sets of worked examples.

5. **Prime student motivation** by connecting topics to students' personal lives and interests, engaging students in collaborative problem solving, and drawing attention to the knowledge and skills students are developing, rather than just using grades or scores.

6. **Use formative assessment** to make learning goals clear to students; continuously monitor, provide feedback, and respond to students' learning progress; and involve students in self- and peer assessment.

Similar recommendations from other reports, such as *Organizing Instruction and Study to Improve Student Learning* (Pashler et al., 2007) and *Top 20 Principles From Psychology for PreK–12 Teaching and Learning* (American Psychological Association, 2015), show consistent findings for instructional strategies that promote learning of skills, conceptual understanding, and problem-solving ability as students actively *do* mathematics in class *with their peers*.

Based on the literature, it is clear that most education professionals agree on the central features of effective mathematics instruction. The following provides a summary of the five critical features of highly effective mathematics lessons you should expect to be part of your child's daily learning experiences in school.

In an effective K–12 mathematics program:

1. Students develop **conceptual understanding** and **procedural skills**.

2. Students **communicate** with peers about mathematics.

3. Students develop **perseverance** and practice mathematics.

4. Students use teacher and peer **feedback** to learn from mistakes.

5. Students use **technology** to support learning.

If your child experiences these five elements in his or her classroom throughout the year, it is likely that he or she is learning and practicing mathematics at a deep level with understanding, which ultimately leads to successful content mastery and college and career readiness by the time he or she graduates from high school.

Students Develop Conceptual Understanding and Procedural Skills

The first thing you should notice is that your child is expected to master skills *and* procedures. But that is no longer sufficient. In a world that puts a premium on the ability to interpret and solve problems, your child also must be able to explain why those procedures work and when they should apply them. This is called *strategic competence*. As outlined in table 2.1 (pages 28–29), for the majority of U.S. history, students have been primarily expected to just memorize and develop basic skills in mathematics class. The emphasis was not on conceptual understanding, problem solving, and strategic competence. However, the CCSS for mathematics and their aligned assessments require students to develop skills based on a foundation of demonstrated conceptual understanding. According to the NRC (Kilpatrick et al., 2001), conceptual understanding

> refers to an integrated and functional grasp of mathematical ideas. Students with conceptual understanding know more than isolated facts and methods. They understand why a mathematical idea is important and the kinds of contexts in

which it is useful. They have organized their knowledge into a coherent whole, which enables them to learn new ideas by connecting those ideas to what they already know. (p. 118)

This likely was not the focus of your own mathematics education and why the nature of the mathematics tasks your child is expected to do in class and at home is changing and needs to change.

Moreover, by expecting your child to understand mathematical concepts that underlie procedures, he or she is more likely to remember the procedures and be able to apply them successfully in new situations (Fuson, Kalchman, & Bransford, 2005). This eventually helps your child become a more effective problem solver.

If students don't *understand* procedures, they sometimes use procedures incorrectly or apply the wrong procedures, which can lead to bizarre results they don't even recognize as bizarre (Martin, 2009). If students learn procedures *with* understanding, it builds a foundation for learning algebraic concepts in middle school and beyond (Carpenter, Franke, & Levi, 2003).

To help you know what it means to learn a procedure with understanding, let's examine a standard every child is expected to learn in elementary school: multiply two two-digit numbers. Suppose someone asked you to multiply forty-three and seventeen—you more than likely learned the traditional algorithm, as shown in figure 4.1. We define an *algorithm* as an approach to solving a problem and not by the specific number of steps or how we record those steps. If completed correctly, the steps lead to the correct answer (the point of an algorithm), but the steps don't necessarily contribute to a student's understanding of the underlying mathematics or build a foundation that contributes to student success in algebra and beyond, thereby making students college and career ready.

$$
\begin{array}{r}
{}^{2}43 \\
\times\ 17 \\
\hline
301 \\
+\ 430 \\
\hline
731
\end{array}
$$

Figure 4.1: Traditional multiplication algorithm.

Your elementary teacher probably explained how to do this problem using strategies similar to those outlined in the following steps. We've indicated in parentheses if the steps are mathematically correct or incorrect. By *incorrect*, we mean that the step is disconnected from any understanding of the mathematical concepts that make the step in the algorithm work (for example, the base-ten positional number system).

1. Multiply 3 and 7 to get 21. (correct)

2. Place the 2 above the 4 and write 1 below. (incorrect)

3. Multiply 7 and 4 to get 28. (incorrect)

4. Add 2 to 28 to get 30. (incorrect)

5. Write 30 next to the 1. (incorrect)

6. Write 0 below the 1. (incorrect)

7. Multiply 1 and 3, and write 3 next to 0. (incorrect)

8. Multiply 1 and 4, and write 4 next to 3. (incorrect)

9. Add 301 and 430 together to get 731. (correct)

Of these nine steps to complete the traditional algorithm, only two are mathematically correct in the sense that completing them reinforces an understanding of mathematical concepts in the problem. Following is a step-by-step breakdown of why the steps labeled *incorrect* are actually mathematically incorrect.

1. What is wrong with step 2? When you place the 2 above the 4, that's not what you are doing mathematically. You aren't really carrying the 2; you are carrying 20 because 3 times 7 is 21.

2. What is wrong with step 3? The first mathematical mistake is that you aren't multiplying 7 and 4, you are actually multiplying 7 and 40. So, the product is actually 280.

3. What is wrong with step 4? You are actually adding 280 and 20 to get 300, not 28 and 2 to get 30.

4. What is wrong with step 5? You aren't actually writing 30, you are writing the result of adding 280 (the product of 7 and 40) to 21 (the product of 3 and 7) to get 301: $7 \times 43 = 301$. While the algorithm eventually results in the correct answer (partial product), it hides how you derive the answer mathematically.

5. What is wrong with step 6? When you were in school, you might have asked your teacher why you write a 0 below the 1 in 301. Your teacher might have told you to "just do it!" The reason this step is necessary in the traditional algorithm is because in the next step, you aren't actually multiplying by 1; you are multiplying by 10. By writing a 0 below the 1 in 301, you are adjusting for the fact that you aren't multiply by a single digit but by a ten (for example, 10, 20, 30). By writing a 0 in the ones place below the first partial product, you can multiply single-digit numbers when completing the steps of the algorithm.

6. What is wrong with step 7? You aren't actually multiplying 1 and 3; you are multiplying 10 and 3 to get 30, not 3. This is why in step 6 your teacher told you to write a 0— this took care of the fact you are actually multiplying by a multiple of ten.

7. What is wrong with step 8? You aren't actually multiplying 1 and 4; you are multiplying 10 and 40 to get 400. When you add this to the 30 you got in step 7, you get the total of 430.

Karen Fuson and Sybilla Beckmann (2012/2013), well-respected mathematics educators who have extensively studied algorithms and the curriculum of high-achieving countries, argue that in order for teachers to teach algorithms effectively and for parents to support those algorithms, they should relate traditional algorithms to visual models.

Visual models (representations) are a critical element of effective math instruction. Effective mathematics teachers utilize drawings or concrete objects (for example, base-ten blocks; see figure 4.2, page 70) to help students make sense of mathematical concepts and procedures, justify their reasoning, and manipulate tools when solving problems (NCTM, 2014). Kilpatrick et al. (2001) write, "Because of the abstract nature of mathematics, people have access to mathematical ideas only through the representations of those ideas" (p. 94).

Your child may have brought home mathematics work in which he or she was asked to draw a picture to justify his or her thinking. This is a perfectly reasonable expectation. Drawing pictures helps students make sense of problems and deepens their understanding. It is important to keep in mind that the drawing is not the goal. The drawing is simply a tool to help students make sense of the mathematics. For example, in figure 4.2, the base-ten blocks provide students with a visual picture of 125 and helps them "see" that 125 is composed of one hundred, two tens, and five ones.

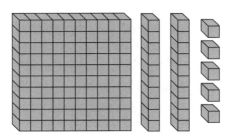

Figure 4.2: Example of base-ten blocks.

Another helpful visual model for students is an open array model, which teachers can use to effectively illustrate the meaning behind the traditional multiplication algorithm. Figure 4.3 shows an open array model of the problem from figure 4.1 (page 67).

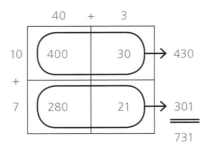

Source: Delise Andrews. Used with permission.

Figure 4.3: Open array model.

This visual model breaks down (decomposes) 43 into 40 and 3, and 17 into 10 and 7. The open array makes it possible to see where all of the partial products come from and emphasizes the place value relationships that allow the traditional algorithm to work. Ultimately, one of the underlying mathematical principles used in the traditional algorithm is a concept you might recall from middle school: the distributive property.

$(40 + 3) (10 + 7) = 40 \times 10 + 40 \times 7 + 3 \times 10 + 3 \times 7 = 731$

The open array model helps students visualize the distributive property at work. They can rely on this understanding—developed when mastering arithmetic procedures—and apply it when they work with algebraic expressions in later grades. Note that this book references traditional arithmetic approaches as *traditional algorithms* and not *standard U.S. algorithms.* You might be surprised to know that most traditional algorithms you learned in school did not originate in the United States. These algorithms emerged in India and were refined by the Persians in the 9th century to make pencil-and-paper calculations efficient (Gullberg, 1997; Wu, 2011).

However, in the successful effort to make algorithms efficient, most of the underlying conceptual understanding (as seen in the open array model for multiplication), has been hidden or removed. Modern machines can carry out these calculations much more efficiently than we can by hand, so our attention can and should shift to focusing on the underlying mathematical concepts (such as place value and the distributive property). That way, students can develop the conceptual foundation and reasoning skills necessary to continue their learning of mathematics.

> *You might be surprised to know that most traditional algorithms you learned in school did not originate in the United States.*

The learning goal is for students to master the efficient traditional multiplication algorithm, precisely because it is efficient, and this is exactly the intent of the CCSS for mathematics. The open array model is merely an *instructional strategy* teachers can employ as they develop student understanding and mastery of the traditional algorithm. Criticism of the Common Core often focuses on instructional strategies, which may be unfamiliar to you as a parent. But it is critical not to confuse instructional strategies with learning goals. The goal (or standard) remains for students to learn the mathematics you learned when you were in school. The difference is that teachers use conceptual instructional strategies, such as the open array model, to build understanding of traditional algorithms.

In the end, this initial approach makes learning the traditional algorithm more meaningful, promotes retention for later grades, and prepares students for further learning in the upper grades. It is also instructionally sound that some students might use a slightly modified but more conceptual version of the traditional algorithm, as shown in figure 4.4, which more clearly illustrates the partial products hidden in the traditional algorithm.

Compare the traditional algorithm in figure 4.1 (page 67) with the more conceptual version in figure 4.4. In figure 4.4, the underlying mathematical concepts of place value and partial products are not hidden as they are in the traditional algorithm. In figure 4.4, we multiply 3 and 7 to get 21, 7 and 40 to get 280, 10 and 3 to get 30, and 10 and 40 to get 400. An additional benefit of the conceptual algorithm is that we don't carry numbers (for example, writing 2 above 4 in figure 4.1, page 67). This lessens the chance of making a procedural error.

$$
\begin{array}{r}
43 \\
\times\ 17 \\
\hline
21 \\
280 \\
30 \\
400 \\
\hline
731
\end{array}
\begin{array}{l}
\\
\\
= 7 \times 3 \\
= 7 \times 40 \\
= 10 \times 3 \\
= 10 \times 40 \\
\end{array}
$$

Figure 4.4: Conceptual version of the traditional multiplication algorithm.

Students Communicate With Peers About Mathematics

When you were in school, your mathematics classroom was most likely a quiet place: the teacher talked, and you listened as you sat in desks aligned in rows. Your teacher probably explained procedures for how to approach the mathematics topic for the day and then demonstrated those procedures by solving example problems for the class. Then you likely worked individually (and quietly), practicing the procedures your teacher modeled. You probably completed this practice alone by working problems out of your textbook or on a worksheet that looked like the examples provided in class.

You should expect your child's mathematics classroom to be less quiet than yours was and filled with purposeful discussions amongst classmates and the teacher about mathematics concepts, skills, and problem-solving strategies. In highly effective mathematics classrooms (by this, we mean high levels of student learning), students engage "mathematics talk" to advance the learning of the whole class (NCTM, 2014). Why? Because

> students who learn to articulate and justify their own mathematical ideas, reason through their own and others' mathematical explanations, and provide a rationale for their answers develop a deep understanding that is critical to their future success in mathematics and related fields. (Carpenter et al., 2003, p. 6)

Of course, for mathematics talk to be highly effective, students must communicate with each other about problems that focus their discussion on reasoning and problem-solving strategies; a strategy most likely to develop a deeper understanding of the content (Michaels, O'Connor, & Resnick, 2008).

Think about the role of discussion in your own life. If you have to explain a concept or idea to someone, you typically need a deep understanding of the subject. If you disagree with someone, either at work or in your personal life, you need a deep understanding of the topic in order to persuade someone that your perspective is the correct lens through which to examine the topic.

Learning mathematics is no different. Students who communicate with their classmates and teacher about their thinking, solution pathways, and insights into how they solved a problem, or who analyze another student's solution, develop a deeper understanding of mathematics. This is why one of the eight mathematical practice standards for the Common Core includes: "Construct viable arguments and critique the reasoning of others" (NGA & CCSSO, 2010, p. 6).

Parents sometimes ask, "Why does my child have to explain how she solved a problem? Isn't it enough that she can just solve it correctly?" The short answer is *no*, it isn't enough! Why? Learning mathematics well is not just about finding the one right answer. The best problems, and most problems in real life, have many solution pathways and sometimes more than a single correct answer. Mathematics also is about the journey

Students who communicate with their classmates and teacher about their thinking, solution pathways, and insights into how they solved a problem, or who analyze another student's solution, develop a deeper understanding of mathematics.

and understanding how to arrive at the destination using multiple pathways. If a student is able to get the right answer, but the solution strategy he or she used is not understood or is flawed, that student might not be able to solve a similar problem again—as a series of mistakes just happened to lead to the correct solution this one time. Or, perhaps the student's solution is based on a misunderstanding that affects the solution to the mathematics task or problem, but he or she lacks understanding and has no idea if his or her answer is correct.

Students need the ability to make sense of solutions to problems that represent their learning of the standards. In fifth grade, for example, the standards require students to use "the meaning of fractions and the meaning of multiplication to multiply a fraction by a whole number" (NGA & CCSSO, 2010, p. 27). In real life, very few people simply take our word for it when we offer a solution to a problem. They want to know *why* our solution is valid as we demonstrate our understanding of the topic or standard.

Imagine you are an engineer who develops a new design for a bridge. A builder or architect is not going to simply trust that your design for the bridge will support the loads it must carry. Before you build the bridge, you must explain (prove) that your design works. In fact, this is largely what professional mathematicians do—they solve problems and develop new mathematical theories. But before those solutions or theories are accepted, mathematicians have to prove (explain) why their solution is valid.

Reflections for **Educators**

Asking questions (prompts) can truly transform a classroom! When a teacher asks questions, it can help him or her determine what students know and encourage them to explain their thinking (NCTM, 2014). Through effective questioning, a highly effective mathematics teacher can create a more interactive environment where students are engaged and persevere by reasoning and thinking about mathematics with their peers and the tasks they are attempting in class together (Walsh & Sattes, 2005).

If you observe your child's mathematics classroom, you should expect the teacher to be asking lots of questions and students to be responding to those questions, questioning each other, and justifying their reasoning and thinking to their classmates and the teacher.

Students Develop Perseverance and Practice Mathematics

Success in mathematics, music, or athletics requires at least one commonality—practice and perseverance! Americans tend to view mathematics ability as something one is either born with or not (you are either a "math person" or you aren't). This simply isn't true (Boaler, 2016). All students can learn more mathematics the same way an athlete improves his or her running time or a musician masters a piece of music—through hard work, corrective feedback (coaching and teaching), and practice, lots of meaningful practice.

Carol Dweck (2006, 2008) has conducted extensive research on what she calls a *fixed mindset*. Individuals with a fixed mindset believe that success in mathematics is a function of innate intelligence or natural ability. The belief that ability is innate is more prevalent in mathematics than it is in other subjects.

Contrast this with a *growth mindset*—the belief that you can become more intelligent through hard work and effort (Dweck, 2006, 2008). Some people have a growth mindset when it comes to music and athletics. You might believe that your child can become a better athlete or a better musician by exerting effort, responding to instruction and feedback (learning from mistakes), trying different strategies, and practicing. Learning mathematics is no different. Everyone can learn more mathematics if they receive high-quality instruction and effective feedback and exert effort that results in corrective practice.

Anyone who becomes an expert at a particular activity or skill must practice in order to develop expertise. Learning mathematics is no different. In an effective mathematics program, students will practice mathematics both in class under the guidance of the teacher and often at home, independently. Both types of practice are critical. By making mistakes during practice, getting

Anyone who becomes an expert at a particular activity or skill must practice in order to develop expertise.

feedback from the teacher, and acting on that feedback, students develop mathematical proficiency and a growth mindset.

In-Class Guided Practice

You should expect your child to struggle at times when learning and practicing mathematics, or reading or writing for that matter. Productive struggle is a natural part of learning both in school and at home when children are practicing mathematics.

To get better at mathematics, your child must practice challenging problems, not just problems that look exactly like the ones shown in class. An athlete only improves when pushed; a musician only develops expertise when a new piece of music is challenging. Jason Moser, Hans Schroder, Carrie Heeter, Tim Moran, and Yu-Hao Lee (2011) confirm that new synapses fire and the brain actually grows when making mistakes during practice. Your child will develop deeper understanding and grow in mathematics learning when he or she practices rigorous problems and makes mistakes that are corrected along the way. Moreover, the nature of mathematics problems (often called *mathematics tasks* in the literature) your child practices in mathematics class and as part of independent practice largely determines what he or she learns (Boston, 2012).

Reflections for Educators

It is critical to support students in persevering when they are confronted with challenges or struggles in mathematics class. Do not let students off the hook when they get stuck on a mathematics problem! Rather, give students scaffolded prompts that encourage them to keep trying. Dweck (2008) states that for the last few decades, many parents and educators have been more focused on "making students feel good about themselves in mathematics and science than in helping them achieve. . . . This may take the form of relieving [students] of the responsibility of doing well, for example, by telling them they are not a 'math person'" (p. 8).

As discussed previously, if the only problems students encounter during mathematics class are routine procedural tasks (for example, in piano lessons, learning only to play the scales), then they will likely only develop procedural skills. If students encounter problems that require them to think, reason, and make sense of mathematics, then they are more likely to develop an understanding of mathematics as well (for example, in piano lessons, learning to play or even create an entire composition versus only playing scales requires an ability to read and interpret music).

In general, students in the United States should practice more types of tasks or mathematics problems that require them to reason and problem solve (Silver, 2010). Ultimately, students retain increased mathematics knowledge when they participate in mathematics lessons requiring them to practice problems that promote thinking, reasoning, and problem solving (Boaler & Staples, 2008).

The concept of perseverance, or *productive struggle* as it is known in the literature (see, for example, NCTM, 2014), during mathematics practice is so critical that it is part of one of the Common Core Mathematical Practices: "Make sense of problems and *persevere* in solving them" (NGA & CCSSO, 2010, p. 6, emphasis added). U.S. students, in general, don't know how to persevere in mathematics. In fact, low levels of student thinking and reasoning across subjects are persistent problems in U.S. education (Kisa & Stein, 2015). Often, the first response of a student stuck during mathematics practice is to quit trying. Effort and perseverance are critical to student learning because students learn more in classrooms where they expend effort and develop perseverance. This happens when teachers resist the urge to water down mathematics standards in an effort to make the work easier for students (Boaler & Staples, 2008).

You can hold your child to the highest levels of expectation when practicing mathematics by not "pushing back" when your child's mathematics teacher expects him or her to understand the mathematics he or she is studying. You also should expect your child to persevere when solving challenging problems that don't look exactly like the ones discussed in class, especially those to be completed outside of class (homework).

In part, you might need to change your beliefs about what effective mathematics teachers do in class. In the United States, many parents and students believe that the job of the mathematics teacher is to make the work easy for students (NCTM, 2014). If, when students are presented with a challenge, the teacher always rescues them by making the task easier, breaking down the

In part, you might need to change your beliefs about what effective mathematics teachers do in class.

task into a series of smaller steps, or telling them exactly what to do, the teacher is actually denying students the opportunity to make sense of mathematics (Stein, Remillard, & Smith, 2007). Such a teaching practice also would unintentionally send students the message that they are not very good at mathematics. This only serves to reinforce a fixed mindset and discourages students from continuing their study of mathematics because they don't believe they have the ability to do it.

We are not advocating that students be needlessly frustrated or experience extreme challenge in the mathematics classroom by being asked to practice difficult mathematics tasks well beyond their current level of understanding. Struggle becomes unproductive when students cannot progress toward understanding or solving problems (Warshauer, 2011).

> We believe you should respond to your child's questions and provide support when he or she becomes stuck. But, you should do so in ways that result in your child continuing to think and reason about mathematics. Students should always be the ones *doing* mathematics practice under your direction and support. They shouldn't simply sit and watch you, his or her teacher, or someone else complete the practice.

Perseverance is a life skill. Your role is to reinforce your child's efforts to learn mathematics and to encourage his or her perseverance during class. Encourage your child to make sense of mathematics and not just focus on the correct answer—understanding *why* is as important as knowing *how. Equilibrium!* Encourage your child to ask questions of their peers and their teacher when they are confused or stuck in class, and emphasize that confusion and making mistakes are a natural part of learning mathematics.

Support your child's teacher, as he or she establishes high expectations for your child to learn mathematics with understanding. Expect your child's teacher to do more than simply spoon-feed your child procedures that he or she is expected to memorize and repeat. In real life, we seldom encounter a problem that is exactly like one we have solved before. We are not expected to solve problems alone. Collaborating with others is an important life skill for your child to learn.

Practice also is necessary to learn mathematics. Once again, the analogy to music and athletics is instructive. Everyone expects musicians and athletes to practice to improve their performance. Learning mathematics is no different. Once your child builds an initial understanding of a mathematics concept or procedure at school (a critical first step), independent practice (homework) can help your child develop mastery and confidence.

Outside-of-Class Independent Practice: Homework

Research indicates that independent practice (homework) can be effective in improving student achievement. In a review of the research on homework, Harris Cooper (2008b) finds a positive relationship between the amount of homework students do and their achievement up to a certain point. Short practice assignments are most effective in the elementary grades, and up to thirty-five to forty minutes of homework appear optimal for high school students (Cooper, 2008a; Fernández-Alonso, Suárez-Álvarez, & Muñiz, 2015). In an effective K–12 mathematics program, you should expect your child to practice mathematics independently nearly every day. However, in the primary grades, students complete much of this independent practice at school.

Short practice assignments are most effective in the elementary grades, and up to thirty-five to forty minutes of homework appear optimal for high school students.

Students need both focused mathematics practice on what they are currently learning and also spaced practice (sometimes called *distributed* or *spiral practice*) to help build retention (Hattie, 2012; Pashler et al., 2007). This means your child may bring home practice on what they learned in school today, but also practice on skills and concepts they learned in previous lessons, the last chapter, or possibly several chapters ago. Homework is most effective if it is assigned regularly and provides a certain level of challenge, without being so difficult that it discourages your child (Fernández-Alonso et al., 2015).

Your role as a parent is not to provide instruction or do the homework for your child. Homework is more effective if your child completes it on his or her own and expends his or her own effort (Fernández-Alonso et al., 2015). In fact, you may want to be cautious offering your child too much help with his or her homework if you are anxious about mathematics yourself. Recent research indicates that when anxious parents frequently help their children with mathematics homework, their children learn significantly less mathematics over a school year and are more likely to develop mathematics anxiety (Maloney, Ramirez, Gunderson, Levine, & Beilock, 2015).

Your role as a parent is to encourage your child to complete his or her homework, re-practice problems that are not yet correct, and ask questions if he or she gets stuck on a problem. If your child becomes significantly frustrated and makes little progress, or the homework seems to take too long, then stop and encourage your child to ask his or her peers for help during practice, interface with online support if possible, or meet with the teacher before class the next day for feedback and support.

> *Your role as a parent is to encourage your child to complete his or her homework, re-practice problems that are not yet correct, and ask questions if he or she gets stuck on a problem.*

Students Use Teacher and Peer Feedback to Learn From Mistakes

As indicated in the previous section, you should expect your child to persevere to make sense of mathematics and solve problems that do not have an immediate or obvious solution. Inside and outside of class, you should expect your child to make mistakes and embrace those mistakes as part of the learning process. You also should expect your child to construct viable arguments with his or her peers, because learning is a collaborative endeavor. Moreover, learning any subject in school also should be part of a *formative learning process*, which includes meaningful and immediate feedback.

Essentially, when learning mathematics, students' experiences should consist of making an effort to solve the mathematics problems presented, possibly making mistakes, embracing those mistakes, and then rethinking solution pathways, carefully checking their solution, and trying again as needed. Much like a child learning to play the piano, this kind of practice occurs both with the teacher during a lesson and without the teacher at home between lessons. So it should be with mathematics practice.

The best mathematics practice uses meaningful feedback and expected action on that feedback as part of a formative learning process. Like any other type of productive practice, whether learning to play the guitar, riding a bicycle, writing a great paragraph, or solving a puzzle, mathematics practice should eventually lead to successful outcomes. The solution pathway—understanding the right strategy or an effective and accurate solution to mathematics problems or tasks—is the result of practice. The ultimate outcome of mathematics practice is for your child to demonstrate learning of the appropriate mathematics standards.

What are the key components of meaningful practice? How can mathematics practice actually lead to improved learning? Your child must receive meaningful feedback during practice. For feedback to be meaningful and helpful, it needs to contain the four components from the FAST acronym: feedback must be fair, accurate, specific, and timely. The FAST acronym is adapted from John Hattie (2009, 2012) and Douglas Reeves (2011).

1. **Fair:** Effective feedback in class, during homework, or after taking a test rests solely on the quality of the work the student demonstrates for the standard, not on characteristics of the student.

2. **Accurate:** Effective feedback acknowledges what students are currently doing well and correctly identifies errors and areas for improvement.

3. **Specific:** Feedback "should be about the particular qualities of [the student's] work, with advice on what he or she can do to improve, and should avoid comparison with other pupils" (Black & Wiliam, 1998, p. 9).

   Feedback should be specific enough that your child can quickly identify the error or logic in his or her reasoning, but not so specific that the teacher makes the corrections. Does test feedback help *students* correct their thinking? If it doesn't, you should discuss this with your child's teacher.

4. **Timely:** Effective feedback is provided in time for students to take formative learning action on input that is immediate and corrective.

Effective and meaningful feedback generally occurs during three stages of the learning process: in class during guided practice, outside of class during independent practice (often at home), and at the end of a unit after tests are returned. Feedback can come from students' peers, their teacher, a tutor, or you.

Stage 1: In-Class Feedback During Guided Practice

Thinking back to the piano lesson analogy, it is not sufficient for your child to simply watch the piano teacher play. The piano teacher must observe your child play and then provide meaningful feedback during guided practice as he or she learns and takes action on any mistakes. The teacher does this in the classroom using small-group discussions to promote conversations about solving mathematics problems during the lesson.

Stage 2: Outside-of-Class Feedback During Independent Practice

Mathematics practice without the teacher is important for the learning process. However, this practice does not need to be done alone. Your child can practice with others, as long as it honors the formative feedback loop. When working on homework, your child should try the problem, check his or her answer or solution for accuracy, and then retry the problem, if incorrect. If your child needs extra feedback or help, then he or she should phone a friend or use a message board, Instagram, or some type of online support tool, if possible, to find help with mathematics practice. Ask your child's teacher how he or she can help you do this.

Stage 3: End-of-Unit Feedback After Tests Are Returned

What happens after your child gets back a mathematics quiz or test from his or her teacher? What is your child asked to do with the mathematics tasks or problems with errors? An end-of-unit quiz or test should allow your child to embrace these errors and reflect on his or her mistakes as well as the standards not yet mastered. Your child should celebrate the standards he or she *has* mastered and then set goals to re-engage in learning the standards that still need improvement.

Consider asking your child's teacher how he or she uses the formative feedback process in class in response to assessments. Make sure you understand the teacher's plan.

Students Use Technology to Support Learning

It is impossible to ignore the reality that the 21st century classroom does not look like the one you might have experienced. Technology integration is here to stay, and it should be embraced as part of meaningful learning experiences.

As a parent, what does this mean for you? How can you help your child find the right balance between pencil-and-paper skills and the technology skills necessary to compete in the digital world?

From a mathematics learning perspective, there are several advantages to integrating 21st century technology into students' learning experiences. The key term, however, is technology *integration*. Technology is not meant for use in isolation away from other elements of mathematics instruction or practice, but rather as a supporting element to mathematics practice and the types of mathematics problems presented in class. The absence of technology in your child's classroom is not good, but the presence of technology is good only if it serves the learning process and is not just a tool used for the sake of using technology.

To be used effectively in the mathematics classroom, technology must help students develop a deeper understanding of mathematics, make sense of mathematical ideas, reason about mathematics, and communicate mathematical thinking (NCTM, 2014). So, what are the benefits of technology use in the 21st century classroom?

> *To be used effectively in the mathematics classroom, technology must help students develop a deeper understanding of mathematics, make sense of mathematical ideas, reason about mathematics, and communicate mathematical thinking.*

First and perhaps foremost, students in 21st century classrooms have the opportunity to learn skills in using technology and other digital tools to solve mathematics problems. The Common Core Standard for Mathematical Practice 5 reads: "Use appropriate tools strategically" (NGA & CCSSO, 2010). This standard requires students to learn when to use various tools, including computers, calculators, and graphing calculators, based on the nature and age appropriateness of the mathematics practice they are expected to do.

For example, Mayer (2009) finds that students learn best when teachers link graphical and linguistic symbols, such as graphs and algebraic symbols. Technology often allows teachers to illustrate mathematical ideas through a dynamic motion or animation lens, which makes the structure of mathematics more evident to students.

Teachers can more thoroughly and clearly develop mathematics concepts for students when they use visual representations of ideas through a graphical interface. For example, if your child is in an algebra 1 course in eighth or ninth grade, you should expect him or her to use a graphing calculator of some form throughout the year. It could be a phone app, an actual calculator, or part of an online resource (many are available at low cost).

A second benefit of the 21st century classroom is the support technology provides for the formative learning process described previously in this chapter. Various types of student response systems allow students and teachers to receive immediate and corrective feedback on practice during class and discover key concepts efficiently and effectively. Additionally, the ability to check student answers during homework online or to go to an online source for feedback on mathematics practice may allow students and teachers to immediately discover gaps in learning.

A third benefit of the 21st century classroom is the use of social media for research and discussion. Within seconds, your child can use and share information about how to proceed and learn about a mathematics problem via social media venues, such as Twitter, Facebook, YouTube, Instagram, Snapchat, Vine, and Spotify. An elementary school district in which one of the authors of this book has worked uses online message boards where upper elementary and middle school students go online every night to receive help from one another with homework practice.

Students become more engaged in mathematics practice because it meets them in an exciting, tech-oriented sharing place, which is more naturally engaging in the Instagram world in which they live.

A fourth benefit of the 21st century classroom is the opportunity for collaborative learning. Your child can use sharing tools, such as Google Classroom, that allow him or her to share diagrams, graphs, explanations, mathematics arguments, and thinking. Students become more engaged in mathematics practice because it meets them in an exciting, tech-oriented sharing place, which is more naturally engaging in the Instagram world in which they live. The most powerful aspect of 1:1 classrooms (classrooms in which every student has a tablet or computer) is the sharing aspect, including immediate feedback for class work and the potential to practice with classmates. The ability to share files and engage in deep collaboration around mathematics concepts brings practice and creativity for that practice to life.

Finally, from a K–12 perspective, every major college readiness assessment your child will take at the state or national level allows for technology integration, such as scientific or graphing calculators. The advent of online-based state and national assessments is expanding rapidly, presenting distinct advantages in the nature of improved problem solving and reasoning for mathematics tasks.

From a K–12 perspective, every major college readiness assessment your child will take at the state or national level allows for technology integration, such as scientific or graphing calculators.

In this chapter, we examined several critical areas of the K–12 student learning experience that can help your child be successful in doing mathematics, including developing conceptual understanding and procedural skills, communicating with peers, expending effort and developing perseverance through mathematics practice, using teacher and peer feedback, and using technology to support learning.

Ultimately, if these learning experiences are present in your child's classroom, your child will go further in learning the expected mathematics standards for his or her grade level, learn more mathematics, and have more options after high school than ever before.

Questions for Reflection

Reflecting on your reading is an opportunity to evaluate and deepen your understanding, gain additional insight, and apply what you have read to your own specific context (Costa & Kallick, 2008). Whether you are an educator or parent, we encourage you to use these questions for personal reflection or to prompt discussion with colleagues and friends if you are reading the book together with the goal of understanding and improving mathematics learning in your local schools.

Questions for Parents

1. Are the learning experiences described in this chapter present in your child's classroom? How do you know? Who might you talk to if you are not sure?

2. Is your child expected to master essential knowledge and skills, develop conceptual understanding, *and* develop the problem-solving skills needed to apply his or her skills and understanding? Ask your child's teacher how he or she does this in mathematics class.

3. Does your child's teacher expect your child to persevere in mathematics class? Do you expect and support this at home? How can you help your child to persevere?

Questions for Educators

1. Is the mathematics program in your classroom, school, or district in a balanced state of equilibrium?

2. Does classroom instruction in your classroom, school, or district emphasize the five critical features of effective instruction outlined in this chapter? How do you know?

3. Do all teachers in your school or district understand and use the features of highly effective mathematics instruction? What professional development support have they had, or do they need, to increase the use of these practices?

Chapter 5

How to Help Your Child Learn Mathematics

While all parents want to find ways to co-educate their children, not all parents know how to do this.

—JOHN HATTIE,
PROFESSOR OF EDUCATION, DIRECTOR OF THE
MELBOURNE EDUCATION RESEARCH INSTITUTE

A s a parent, you are your child's first teacher, and you are in a prime position to have a significant influence on his or her academic development. Through the values you communicate about education, effort, persistence, and responsibility, you influence your child's mathematics achievement.

With respect to mathematics, Nancy Kober (1991) asserts that parental attitudes toward mathematics are a good predictor of children's mathematics achievement at all grade levels. As she notes, "Children's self-concept and confidence in their own mathematics aptitude is more directly related to their parents' perceptions of their competence than to children's own achievement record" (Kober, 1991, p. 47).

With this in mind, we believe you should always talk about mathematics in positive ways. Regardless of your mathematics background or experiences, let your child know that learning mathematics well is an important life skill. Communicating a positive "can do" attitude and message about mathematics promotes your child's success. Your child is a mirror—he or she reflects back to you exactly the mindset you present to him or her. If you complain or say you hated mathematics in school, your child will most likely reflect that mindset back to you and his or her teacher.

Above all, support and encourage your child's efforts to use processes and strategies that can lead to problem solving in mathematics, not his or her talent or ability. With proper and focused effort, your child can learn mathematics. Dweck (2006, 2008) makes it clear that when parents praise their children's *efforts* toward reasonable solution strategies, their children are more likely to try more rigorous mathematics problems in class. When parents (or teachers, for that matter) praise students for their mathematics *talent*, the students are more likely to shut down and not try more challenging problems in class. Thus, encouraging your child to try hard every day to learn appropriate processes for developing his or her mathematical reasoning is a good start for mathematics success.

As a parent, you should obtain basic information about your child's mathematics class. This includes copies of course or grade-level outlines, homework assignments for each unit, the intent of and vision for mathematics instruction in your child's school, and other materials that may assist you in understanding your child's mathematics program.

There are two specific questions you can ask your child's mathematics teacher as you support constructive parental involvement with him or her and the mathematics program.

1. How will mathematics look in my child's classroom?

2. How can I help my child with mathematics practice at home?

How Will Mathematics Look in My Child's Classroom?

First and foremost, you need specific information about what mathematics instruction "looks like," with special attention to those aspects that are most different from what you experienced as a student. You should advocate for a mathematics classroom with an instructional emphasis as outlined in chapter 4 of this book.

Figure 5.1 provides seven questions you can ask yourself and your child's teacher as you examine your child's learning experiences at various grade levels. Answers to these questions will reveal if the instructional strategies advocated for in this book are present in your child's classroom (Kanold et al., 2012).

These questions can act as a resource for your child's school and the current efforts of its mathematics program. To obtain the answers to these questions, you may ask a teacher leader at your child's school, or ask your child's teacher directly how he or she specifically responds to these questions in class.

---

1. **Is my child expected to know both essential arithmetic skills and the mathematical concepts at the foundation of these skills?**

   - Is my child learning and applying basic computational skills and learning about the properties of operations and relationships in our number system so he or she understands why computational procedures work?

   - Is my child creating informal ways to solve computation problems using properties of operations and knowledge of the base-ten number system and using a variety of algorithms to build understanding of more standard procedures for adding, subtracting, multiplying, and dividing multidigit numbers? Is my child using multiple representations, such as drawings and graphs, to support his or her solutions to mathematics problems?

2. **Is my child doing more than arithmetic and basic mathematics facts?**

   - Does my child see mathematics as much more than arithmetic (knowing the facts and number operations), including estimation, geometry, probability, data analysis, algebra, and more?

3. **Is my child striving to achieve high standards and being assessed regularly to determine his or her progress?**

   - Do the students in my child's school achieve high levels of performance on the standards for understanding, complexity, and accuracy that the teachers, school, and state set for them?

4. **Is my child solving challenging problems to learn new mathematical ideas, concepts, and skills?**

   - Does my child complete challenging tasks designed to help him or her investigate new ideas? Do I see my child discuss and write explanations for his or her thinking with classmates and the teacher?

Source: Adapted from Kanold et al., 2012.

Figure 5.1: Mathematics instructional strategies tool.

Continued →

5. **Is my child working with other students?**

- Is my child sometimes collaborating in class and during homework time to make discoveries, draw conclusions, and discuss mathematics concepts and operations as he or she tries and retries problems?

6. **Is my child's knowledge and understanding evaluated in a variety of ways?**

- Is my child's teacher using many different ways to determine if he or she knows and understands mathematics concepts? Do some of these ways include open-ended questions for which my child writes out the steps—or thought processes—used in solving mathematics problems, independent and group projects, and other written tests?

- Is my child allowed to re-engage with mathematics problems for standards in which he or she consistently shows weakness?

7. **Is my child learning to use technology appropriately?**

- Is my child using a calculator as a tool (not a crutch) for performing operations with large numbers or complex graphs, knowing that using a calculator should not replace a thorough knowledge of basic mathematics operations or an essential understanding of the functions?

- Is my child using computer applications and online resources that pose interesting mathematical situations that would not be available to him or her without the technology?

Also, note that while you may remember taking multiple-choice tests in mathematics class, you may be unfamiliar with modern mathematics performance assessments, mathematics testing in an online environment, or especially the nature of the assessments for the types of mathematics questions developed for Common Core–type state standards. You may want to go online and examine the nature of current online testing as well as online support for homework tasks and more.

We know you want to help your child learn mathematics successfully. However, helping your child will be different than your own experiences, as routine answers to mathematics problems are not as applicable. Your child's mathematics experiences will emphasize completing high-level tasks and developing conceptual understanding, thinking, and reasoning. Following are some basic suggestions for how you can help your child with mathematics practice at home.

Reflections for **Educators** ═══════════════════

You can use the mathematics instructional strategies tool as a way to evaluate the quality of your current mathematics program and whether or not it is meeting the needs of students and parent expectations. Invite a variety of stakeholders, including parents, teachers, and students, to work collaboratively to respond to these high expectations for your mathematics program.

You also should evaluate the quality of parent involvement in your school. How do you currently explain to parents what their children are learning in your school? How do you communicate new expectations for learning mathematics in your school? Are you taking an active approach? Are parents welcome to question the nature of learning mathematics in the classroom each day?

How Can I Help My Child With Mathematics Practice at Home? PreK–5

There are many ways you can make mathematics part of your family's daily life. Yes, children learn mathematics at school, but parents play a critical role at home as well. This is especially true in the early years. You can give your child a great start in mathematics by helping him or her learn to count before reaching kindergarten. From ages two to four, simply helping your child understand the meaning of *how many* can give him or her a significant jumpstart. You can read counting books with your child, help him or her to count by playing games, or sing counting songs together. Use the real world around you to count items that just naturally occur, such as toys, stairs, dolls, plates, cookies, days on a calendar, rows in a garden, or keys.

By the end of fifth grade, successful learning of the progression of topics for elementary school should include fluency in three critical areas (NGA & CCSSO, 2010, p. 33).

1. Addition, subtraction, and multiplication of fractions

2. Extending division to two-digit divisors and understanding decimal operations

3. Developing understanding and use of volume

Figure 5.2 offers several ways you can support your child's early mathematics learning.

---

1. **Help your child develop automatic recall of basic facts.**
   Although it is important that students learn the meaning underlying basic addition, subtraction, multiplication, and division facts first, it is ultimately important for them to develop immediate fact recall. Immediate recall is a function of practice, and there is limited time in the school day for such practice. You can use basic fact practice as an opportunity to help your child learn. Note that this practice does not require any materials. Orally presenting facts promotes immediate recall better than worksheets. Perfect times to practice are while driving, walking, bike riding, waiting in line, and so on.

2. **Play games.** Games are a great way to practice mathematics concepts and skills and also promote positive parent-child relationships. Both traditional board games, but also the wide variety of online games and apps now available, can make math practice fun and engaging for your child. You can go to www.parents.com to find some great recommendations for your child.

3. **Provide support with problem solving.** Because your child will work on complex problems at home, use these questioning strategies to help him or her without solving the problems yourself.

   - What is the problem asking you to find out?

   - What does the problem tell you?

   - Can you tell me the problem in your own words?

   - Is there anything you don't understand? Where can you find answers to your questions?

   - What will you try first? Next?

   - Will it help to draw a picture or graph? Act it out? Make a list?

   - How do you know if your answer or solution method is correct?

   - What do you estimate the answer will be?

   - Have you ever worked a problem like this before?

Figure 5.2: Supporting student mathematics learning at home.

4. **Find mathematics everywhere.** Mathematics problems are part of everyday life. Encourage and engage your child to solve everyday problems as they arise. The appendix in *Helping Your Child Learn Mathematics* (U.S. Department of Education, 2005) has many suggestions for such problems.

5. **Monitor your attitude.** What is your own attitude toward mathematics? Parents who communicate ideas such as, "Math is hard," "It's OK that you're not doing well in mathematics," or "I never did well in mathematics either" promote attitudes that are counterproductive to their children's success. Instead, give messages consistent with the belief that success in mathematics comes from hard work and effort; it's something everyone can do; and it's important to do well in mathematics to be prepared for the future.

6. **Support lots of practice at home.** Practice is a necessary part of learning mathematics. Encourage your child to complete his or her practice, but do so without actually doing the homework for him or her. Give your child feedback on how he or she is doing on homework, and then encourage him or her to take action if it is not correct.

7. **Talk to your child about mathematics.** Talk to your child about the ways you use mathematics. Talk about mathematics when you are shopping, making various decisions, and when you see mathematics in news stories you read or see.

8. **Constantly ask your child, "Why?" and "How do you know?"** These simple questions reinforce the importance of understanding and justifying one's work.

Through these learning progressions, students are prepared for the expectations of middle school mathematics, including the study of ratios and proportions as well as statistics, geometry, and algebra. You can visit **go.solution-tree.com/MathematicsatWork** to download free reproducibles of figures 5.1 and 5.2.

How Can I Help My Child With Mathematics Practice at Home? Middle School

Let's take a deeper look at item 6 from the list in figure 5.2: support lots of practice at home. As your child grows older and progresses to middle school, you may begin to worry that you do not know or understand the mathematics he or she is studying. Or, you may not know the methods his or her teacher is using for instruction. Here is the good news: because homework is really just additional mathematics practice after a lesson in school (like additional practice after a music lesson), your primary role is to ensure your child perseveres through the practice. You can make sure your child has a good place to practice. You can check in from time to time to see how your child is doing. Is he or she practicing well? Is your child correcting errors as he or she practices?

Reflections for **Educators**

During curriculum nights or parent-teacher conferences, be sure to emphasize the importance of parents praising their child's efforts and perseverance in addition to correct answers. Share your course or grade-level syllabus and learning objectives with parents so they are aware of what their children are learning when in your classroom.

You also can ask the questions from figure 5.2, item 3 (page 92) or use prompts that help your child trigger a memory from class earlier that day, such as:

- "How can you organize what you know about this problem?"
- "How might you begin? What is a good way to get started?"
- "Can you show me the strategy you used to complete the problem?"
- "Does your answer make sense to you?"
- "Convince me that your solution makes sense."
- "Do you see any patterns in the problem?"
- "Would a table, diagram, or picture of the problem help you?"
- "Can you phone a friend? Who might be able to help you?"
- "Is there a mathematics technology tool you can use, such as a computer or calculator? If you used the technology tool, does your answer make sense?"
- "Is there online help available through your textbook or a homework help line?"

The most important aspect of practice in middle school mathematics is that your child does the practice correctly, re-correcting any errors he or she makes. Your role is to make sure your child is persevering through the practice and can show you evidence that the practice is complete.

The Internet also can be an excellent source of support for students' mathematics practice and to inform your understanding of the mathematics your child is studying. Ask your child's teacher for some reliable online resources to support expected mathematics practice in your child's specific mathematics curriculum. Online sources—both video and in print—can be a great support as you help your child understand the mathematics he or she is learning in school.

How Can I Help My Child With Mathematics Practice at Home? High School

Regardless of your high school mathematics experiences, successfully learning algebra concepts—including building functions, statistics, and geometry—are essential to college- and career-ready opportunities by the time your child graduates high school.

The nature of the algebra curriculum is served by K–8 mathematics experiences that nurture number fluency, fraction proficiency, and an understanding of patterns and functions. Algebra is not a capstone course but the fundamental building block course to all high school mathematics.

Just like elementary school, high school also has state standards that your local school district is obligated to meet. These standards cover a wide range of content that allows your child to become college and career ready. In order to meet these standards, schools must offer at least three years of mathematics, with algebra 1 as the beginning course. This means your child must take and successfully complete three years of high school mathematics at a minimum. These courses can help your child be better prepared for college entrance exams. Most states test your child in mathematics at the end of his or her junior year, if not sooner, or in some cases more often.

You can help your high school student by finding out what he or she is required to learn in each course, making sure he or she is doing the practice required by the teacher and staying positive even when the work seems difficult.

You also should expect your child's high school principal to provide meaningful intervention and support to help ensure your child's success in mathematics classes. Meaningful intervention might include before, during, or after school homework help, videos of teachers' lessons available online, or required interventions, as needed.

You can help by making sure your child is in class every day and on time, working with the teacher as soon as your child starts to struggle in class, and volunteering whenever possible at the school. You also can help by asking your child the questions listed on page 94. Be sure to advocate for your child when needed, and teach your child how to advocate for him or herself first, especially as he or she gets older. Work with the school counselor, school advisory group, and other school support staff, if needed. Ask lots of questions, and share your concerns if you think your child needs more help or direction in mathematics class.

Reflections for **Educators**

Review item 3 in figure 5.2 (page 92). How does your school mathematics program support parents in asking these questions at home? How does your current parent communication process allow for the development of parent and teacher understanding of these critical questions as part of student learning and perseverance when practicing mathematics?

Your child's K–12 journey as a mathematics student is filled with increasingly more difficult challenges as each year progresses. At some point along the way, the standards for the mathematics he or she is learning may outpace your own knowledge. However, this does not diminish your role or your responsibility to ensure that your child is learning, making the effort needed to persevere, and seeking help when experiencing difficulties.

Remember, you can support your child by monitoring your own attitude about mathematics. Parents who understand the importance of deliberate and ongoing mathematics practice as part of homework, concentration without social media distraction, and the difference between superficial understanding and deep understanding of mathematics are most likely to nurture successful mathematics learning experiences in school and at home.

Questions for Reflection

Reflecting on your reading is an opportunity to evaluate and deepen your understanding, gain additional insight, and apply what you have read to your own specific context (Costa & Kallick, 2008). Whether you are an educator or parent, we encourage you to use these questions for personal reflection or to prompt discussion with colleagues and friends if you are reading the book together with the goal of understanding and improving mathematics learning in your local schools.

Questions for Parents

1. Reflect on how you communicate about mathematics at home. Is it positive and with a "can do" attitude, or is it more negative? How could you improve this communication?

2. How can you help your child persevere during mathematics practice at home? Do you focus on effort and help him or her learn how to get unstuck if needed?

3. Does your child's curriculum offer online resources and support that you and your child can access? Who can you ask at the school to provide these resources for you?

Questions for Educators

1. How can you better communicate the parent support strategies in this chapter to all parents?

2. Do your students' parents, the school, and the district understand your expectations for mathematics learning in your school? How do you know? Does your school offer interventions (for example, extra instructional or tutoring time) to support students who struggle with mathematics?

3. Have you discussed the importance of developing a growth mindset with parents? How do you focus parents on the importance of student effort on a daily basis?

Epilogue

Conclusion and Action Steps for Educators and Parents

Regardless of how difficult you think it is to improve classroom mathematics teaching on a wide scale, it is more difficult than that.

—JAMES HIEBERT,
PROFESSOR, SCHOOL OF EDUCATION,
UNIVERSITY OF DELAWARE

Although many aspects of mathematics education in society must change for us to achieve the vision of teaching and learning that all students deserve and the United States needs, we believe a critical strategy in achieving this vision is for both educators *and* parents to support and advocate for an equilibrium experience in classrooms, schools, and districts. This includes supporting more rigorous and common mathematics standards for *all* students and implementing effective instructional strategies, as outlined in chapter 4.

If we know what effective mathematics instruction is, why is it so hard to implement (and accept) in the classroom? James Hiebert (2013), a highly respected mathematics educator at the University of Delaware, offers a couple of explanations, including the following.

- Disagreement on mathematics learning goals
- Cultural nature of mathematics teaching

Disagreement on Mathematics Learning Goals

As discussed in chapter 2, there has been a fundamental disagreement on two issues in the history of mathematics education (Jones & Coxford, 1970).

1. What should be the nature of mathematics that students learn—facts, skills, and procedures, or concepts and understanding?

2. How should students learn mathematics—teacher directed with a focus on memorization, or student centered through reasoning and discovery?

Disagreement on the answers to these questions persists today and lies at the heart of the debate over the Common Core and most conflicts in mathematics education.

But at a certain level, with respect to standards and expectations, mathematics is mathematics. Fractions and decimals are no different in California than they are in Maine. There is no reason why fourth graders in Florida shouldn't be learning the same material about fractions as fourth graders in Oregon. And as we have made perfectly clear, students should be procedurally fluent with fractions, understand the underlying concepts of *why* fraction procedures work, and be able to draw on both to solve problems. Teaching for conceptual understanding and skill mastery are not opposing forces; they support and strengthen one another in an appropriate state of equilibrium.

The CCSS for mathematics define a common expectation for student learning in mathematics. These standards are coherent, focused, and based on what we know about the appropriate sequencing of mathematics topics to promote student learning—both from the research on learning progressions and through international comparisons. In addition, the CCSS for mathematics call for equilibrium: "Mathematical understanding and procedural skill are equally important" (NGA & CCSSO, 2010, p. 4).

The CCSS for mathematics call for equilibrium.

There is a clear need to teach mathematics at a deeper level so students understand the underlying concepts and are able to transfer their understanding and skills to solve problems. The CCSS for mathematics emphasize the deeper learning of mathematics and represent a set of mathematical standards that can help us accomplish this goal of deeper learning for all students (NRC, 2012a).

You can look at the CCSS for mathematics or any set of similar standards this way: high-quality standards call for students to learn the mathematics you learned when you were in school (although a lot more mathematics in addition to what you learned!). High-quality standards call for students to understand mathematics at a deep level and be able to use that understanding to solve problems. That's it—know *how* (procedural skill), know *why* (conceptual understanding), and know *when* (application)—the very definition of rigor in the Common Core (CCSSI, 2010). There is no reason that should be controversial.

Cultural Nature of Mathematics Teaching

As we have discussed throughout this book, teaching is a cultural activity—mathematics teaching, in particular (Hiebert, 2013). As Hiebert (2013) writes, this means that the instructional strategies for teaching mathematics

> are not invented new by each teacher. Methods of teaching are handed down from one generation to the next. . . . [Teachers] acquire their training by observing what their teachers do. . . . The methods they use to teach—the ways in which they interact with students around content—are likely to be determined by their own experiences as students in K–12 classrooms. (p. 52)

Hiebert refers to how mathematics teachers learn to teach and develop their beliefs concerning effective mathematics instruction. (See also *The Teaching Gap: Best Ideas from the World's Teachers for Improving Education in the Classroom* [Stigler & Hiebert, 1999].) We contend this argument also applies to all adults in the United States. We all have a preconceived notion as to what we believe we should see in the mathematics classroom and what we believe constitutes effective mathematics instruction.

Most adults in the United States have experienced classroom mathematics instruction. In fact, most high school graduates have experienced about 1,500 hours of mathematics instruction. This creates a powerful cultural expectation for mathematics teaching and

Most high school graduates have experienced about 1,500 hours of mathematics instruction.

learning among the general public that does not exist for other professions. Let's consider a physician. Most physicians in the United States did not grow up during their formative years observing a physician at work for one hundred eighty days per year for thirteen straight years. Consequently, we do not have the same sort of expectation for how a physician does his or her job that we do for mathematics teachers. Therefore, we trust the professional expertise of the physician who is treating us and, in fact, expect that our physician is up to date with current research and treatment protocols. When physicians use the latest and most effective research-informed treatment protocols, most of us do not push back and demand that they instead treat us with leeches.

And yet, because mathematics teaching and learning is a cultural activity, we do resist change. This is natural, as cultures exist in part to resist change—to pass on current practices and beliefs to the next generation (Stigler & Thompson, 2009). However, this also impedes progress toward improving mathematics teaching and learning. Often, when educators, schools, and districts attempt to implement research-informed practices, including some of the research-informed instructional strategies we have outlined here, some parents (as well as some educators) resist that change because it doesn't conform to their beliefs and cultural expectations for mathematics teaching and learning.

Because mathematics teaching and learning is a cultural activity, we do resist change.

As a result, as James Stigler and Belinda Thompson (2009) argue, we are still conducting certain aspects of mathematics instruction as we have for centuries, even though the importance of mathematics education to students' future success, what we know about teaching and learning mathematics, and the students themselves have all dramatically changed. You wouldn't want your physician to treat you the way physicians would have treated their patients decades or even centuries ago. The same should be true with respect to our expectations for mathematics teaching and learning.

As educators and parents, how can we overcome the inertia of the past so students receive a mathematics education that likely differs from the one we received ourselves and graduate mathematically proficient and college and career ready? There are some definite action steps we can take.

Action Steps

It is essential that we no longer debate the merits of either the CCSS for mathematics or any other set of coherent, comprehensive, and rigorous standards. Instead, we now have the opportunity to use standards that require a balance of procedural fluency with complex reasoning as a catalyst to raise expectations for student learning and support effective instructional practices in the classroom. William Schmidt (2012) writes:

> The Common Core [standards] offer the opportunity to revolutionize math instruction in this country, to improve student performance, to close the gap between the United States and its competitors, and to ensure that every American student has an equal opportunity to learn important mathematics content. But it is only a chance, and it is imperative that we seize it. (p. 25)

How can educators and parents seize this opportunity? Following are six action steps you can take to support improved mathematics teaching and learning in your school, no matter what set of standards your state or school district has adopted.

1. Advocate for higher mathematics expectations. This includes supporting the implementation of more rigorous and common mathematics content and process standards.

2. Advocate for the implementation of the research-informed instructional strategies described in chapter 4.

3. Expect and support students' perseverance when they work on challenging mathematics tasks. Make it your goal that students develop a growth mindset.

4. Expect students to develop both conceptual understanding and procedural fluency, and the ability to draw on both to solve problems—learning *how, why,* and *when.* Advocate and support this expectation in your school.

5. Support the appropriate use of assessment (testing) to identify students' strengths and weaknesses, and encourage your school to use that information to support continued learning.

Continued →

6. Be willing to confront individuals who criticize mathematics education based on little more than Internet innuendo and half-truths. Discuss education issues from an informed point of view based on evidence and the literature. Expect others to do the same. Ignore those who don't.

Most of all, it is time we stop complaining! Thames and Ball (2013) write, "Americans have long complained about the quality of mathematics education" (p. 15). We know what mathematics our students should learn in school as well as what constitutes the effective mathematics instruction necessary to support that learning. We have illustrated what effective mathematics instruction is and why it is important. "If the discourse ten years from now is to be something other than a refrain about why U.S. mathematics education does not work, a different strategy is needed" (Thames & Ball, 2013, p. 15). We believe the equilibrium position is that necessary different strategy and the best way forward for our students' mathematics education and future success.

> *We believe the equilibrium position is that necessary different strategy and the best way forward for our students' mathematics education and future success.*

We believe mathematics teaching and learning *must* be improved. We believe mathematics teaching and learning *can* be improved. We believe we know *how* it can be improved. We believe educators and parents are critical partners in the effort to improve what our students learn and how they learn it, so that *all* students graduate from high school prepared for either a career or to further their education. The future of the United States depends on it.

We encourage educators and parents to work together to balance the mathematics education equation and make equilibrium in the mathematics learning experience a reality for all students and generations to come!

Appendix:
Additional Resources for Parents

This appendix provides an annotated list of additional resources parents might find useful as they support their child's mathematics learning. The resources include print materials to further their understanding of mathematics education, online games, and websites offering additional mathematics sources.

Figure This! (http://figurethis.nctm.org): NCTM developed this resource to help families enjoy mathematics outside of school through a series of fun and engaging, high-quality challenges. Check out the Family Corner for tips on helping your child with mathematics.

Gamequarium (www.gamequarium.org/dir/Gamequarium /Math): This free web resource provides grade-level practice for all mathematics standards and supports student practice at home for additional skill building.

***Helping Your Child Learn Mathematics* (U.S. Department of Education, 2005) (www2.ed.gov/parents/academic/help/math /math.pdf):** This free guide discusses what it means to be a problem solver, communicate mathematically, and demonstrate reasoning ability. It also includes many suggestions for activities you can use to help your child develop mathematics skills. The activities are arranged by level of difficulty and grade level and include a tip box as well as an explanation of the mathematics concept behind each activity. It includes a reference list of mathematics-related resources, including websites, books, computer software, and magazines.

Hooda Math (www.hoodamath.com): This web resource provides hundreds of online games and competitions students can play appropriate to their grade level or mathematics course. It is free and provides additional opportunities for mathematics practice to deepen understanding of concepts in each grade level.

Internet4Classrooms (www.internet4classrooms.com): This web resource provides games and lessons for helping students and parents understand mathematics standards for each grade level in K–12.

Page 1 of 3

***It's Elementary: A Parent's Guide to K–5 Mathematics* (Whitenack, Cavey, & Henney, 2015):** This book helps you to understand elementary-level mathematics and instructional strategies in jargon-free language.

Khan Academy (www.khanacademy.org): Khan Academy provides video mathematics lessons on a variety of topics. These videos can provide a supplementary resource and 24/7 tutoring.

LearnZillion (www.learnzillion.com): LearnZillion provides videos that provide conceptual development and practice for all grade levels and mathematics courses. This website provides great tutorials for parents as well.

Math Forum (http://mathforum.org): Have a mathematics question? Ask Dr. Math at the Math Forum. You or your child can pose a question or browse the extensive archive of previously asked questions and responses.

The National Council of Teachers of Mathematics (NCTM) (www.nctm.org): Founded in 1920, NCTM is the world's largest mathematics education organization. NCTM is the public voice of mathematics education, dedicated to ensuring all students receive the highest quality mathematics education. The NCTM website contains a wealth of information and resources for both educators and parents.

***A Parent's Guide to Helping Your Child With Today's Math* (National Education Association, n.d.) (www.nea.org/assets /docs/HE/44013_NEA_W_L9.pdf):** This web resource explains how current mathematics instruction differs from instruction in the past and offers suggestions for ways you can help your child with mathematics.

Teaching and Learning Mathematics With the Common Core (www.nctm.org/Standards-and-Positions/Common-Core -State-Standards/Teaching-and-Learning-Mathematics-with-the -Common-Core): NCTM and the Hunt Institute produced a series of videos designed to help you understand the mathematics your child requires to be successful in the early years through high school to prepare for college, life, and careers. The videos examine why developing conceptual understanding requires a different approach to teaching and learning than you likely experienced as a student.

The video topics include:

- Building conceptual understanding for mathematics
- Mathematics in the early grades
- Developing mathematical skills in upper elementary grades
- Mathematical foundations for success in algebra
- Preparation for higher-level mathematics
- Standards for mathematical practice
- Parents supporting mathematics learning

What's Math Got to Do With It?: How Teachers and Parents Can Transform Mathematics Learning and Inspire Success **(Boaler, 2015):** In this inspiring book, Stanford University professor Jo Boaler reviews research on the brain and mathematics learning and provides practical suggestions for supporting student learning.

YouCubed at Stanford University (http://youcubed.org): This Stanford University website provides free resources for both teachers and parents.

References and Resources

Achenbach, J. (2015). The age of disbelief. *National Geographic, 227*(3), 30–47.

Achieve. (2015, May). *Proficient vs. prepared: Disparities between state tests and the 2013 National Assessment of Educational Progress (NAEP).* Washington, DC: Author. Accessed at www.achieve.org/files /NAEPBriefFINAL051415.pdf on August 24, 2015.

ACT. (2015). *The condition of college and career readiness 2015: National.* Iowa City, IA: Author.

Aguirre, J., Mayfield-Ingram, K., & Martin, D. B. (2013). *The impact of identity in K–8 mathematics: Rethinking equity-based practices.* Reston, VA: National Council of Teachers of Mathematics.

American Psychological Association. (2015). *Top 20 principles from psychology for preK–12 teaching and learning.* Accessed at www.apa.org /ed/schools/cpse/top-twenty-principles.pdf on August 24, 2015.

America's Promise Alliance. (2015). *High school graduation facts: Ending the dropout crisis.* Accessed at www.americaspromise.org/high-school -graduation-facts-ending-dropout-crisis on October 7, 2015.

Atler, C. (2014, March 26). Dad's rant about common core math problem goes viral. *Time.* Accessed at time.com/38816/dads-rant-about -common-core-math-problem-goes-viral/ on January 25, 2016.

Autor, D. H. (2014). Skills, education, and the rise of earnings inequality among the "other 99 percent." *Science, 344*(6186), 843–851.

Ball, D. L., Ferrini-Mundy, J., Kilpatrick, J., Milgram, R. J., Schmid, W., & Schaar, R. (2005). Reaching for common ground in K–12 mathematics education. *Notices of the AMS, 52*(9), 1055–1058.

Bandeira de Mello, V., Bohrnstedt, G., Blankenship, C., & Sherman, D. (2015, June). *Mapping state proficiency standards onto the NAEP scales: Results from the 2013 NAEP reading and mathematics assessments* (NCES 2015-046). Washington, DC: National Center for Education Statistics. Accessed at http://nces.ed.gov/nationsreportcard/subject/publications /studies/pdf/2015046.pdf on July 12, 2015.

Black, P., & Wiliam, D. (1998). *Inside the black box: Raising standards through classroom assessment.* London: Assessment Group of the British Educational Research Association.

Boaler, J. (2015). *What's math got to do with it?: How teachers and parents can transform mathematics learning and inspire success.* New York: Penguin.

Boaler, J. (2016). *Mathematical mindsets: Unleashing students' potential through creative math, inspiring messages and innovative teaching.* San Francisco, CA: Jossey-Bass.

Boaler, J., & Staples, M. (2008). Creating mathematical futures through an equitable teaching approach: The case of Railside School. *Teachers College Record, 110*(3), 608–645.

Boston, M. (2012). Assessing instructional quality in mathematics. *Elementary School Journal, 113*(1), 76–104.

Botham, P. E. B. (1832). *The common school arithmetic.* Hartford, CT: Benton.

Bridge, B. (1831). *The southern and western calculators, or elements of arithmetic: Adapted to the currency of the United States, for use in schools.* Philadelphia: Key, Mielke, Biddle.

Brownell, W. A. (1935). Psychological considerations in the learning and the teaching of arithmetic. In W. D. Reeve (Ed.), *The teaching of arithmetic* (10th yearbook of the National Council of Teachers of Mathematics, pp. 1–31). New York: Bureau of Publications, Teachers College, Columbia University.

Camera, L. (2015, July 30). *Conference process to re-write ESEA gets underway* [Blog post]. Accessed at http://blogs.edweek.org/edweek /campaign-k-12/2015/07/conference_process_to_rewrite_.html on October 9, 2015.

Carnevale, A. P., Cheah, B., & Hanson, A. R. (2015). *The economic value of college majors.* Washington, DC: Center on Education and the Workforce, Georgetown University. Accessed at https://cew.georgetown .edu/wp-content/uploads/The-Economic-Value-of-College-Majors-Full -Report-Web.compressed.pdf on August 24, 2015.

Carpenter, T. P., Franke, M. L., & Levi, L. (2003). *Thinking mathematically: Integrating arithmetic and algebra in elementary school*. Portsmouth, NH: Heinemann.

Castillo, C., Mendoza, M., & Poblete, B. (2011). Information credibility on Twitter. In *Proceedings of the 20th International Conference on World Wide Web* (pp. 675–684). New York: Association for Computing Machinery.

Chingos, M. M. (2015). *Breaking the curve: Promises and pitfalls of using NAEP data to assess the state role in student achievement*. Washington, DC: Urban Institute. Accessed at www.urban.org/sites/default/files /alfresco/publication-pdfs/2000484-Breaking-the-Curve-Promises-and -Pitfalls-of-Using-NAEP-Data-to-Assess-the-State-Role-in-Student -Achievement.pdf on October 27, 2015.

Cohen, P. C. (2003). Numeracy in nineteenth-century America. In G. M. A. Stanic & J. Kilpatrick (Eds.), *A history of school mathematics* (Vol. 1, pp. 43–76). Reston, VA: National Council of Teachers of Mathematics.

Colburn, W. (1821). *An arithmetic on the plan of Pestalozzi*. Boston: Cummings and Hilliard.

Colburn, W. (1826). *Colburn's first lessons: Intellectual arithmetic, upon the inductive method of instruction*. Boston: Reynolds.

College Board. (2014). *Program summary report*. New York: Author. Accessed at http://media.collegeboard.com/digitalServices/pdf /research/2014/Prog-Summary-Report-2014.pdf on October 9, 2015.

College Board. (2015a). *2015 college-bound seniors: Total group profile report*. New York: Author.

College Board. (2015b). *Annual results reveal largest and most diverse group of students take PSAT/NMSQT®, SAT®, and AP®; need to improve readiness remains*. Accessed at www.collegeboard.org/releases/2015/annual-results -reveal-largest-most-diverse-group-students-take-psat-sat-ap on October 1, 2015.

Commission on Mathematics. (1959). *Program for college preparatory mathematics*. New York: College Entrance Examination Board.

Common Core State Standards Initiative. (2010). *Key shifts in mathematics*. Accessed at www.corestandards.org/other-resources/key -shifts-in-mathematics/ on December 12, 2015.

Cooper, H. (2008a). *Effective homework assignments* (Research brief). Reston, VA: National Council of Teachers of Mathematics.

Cooper, H. (2008b). *Homework: What the research says* (Research brief). Reston, VA: National Council of Teachers of Mathematics.

Costa, A. L., & Kallick, B. (2008). Learning through reflection. In A. L. Costa & B. Kallick (Eds.), *Learning and leading with habits of mind: Sixteen essential characteristics for success* (pp. 221–235). Alexandria, VA: Association for Supervision and Curriculum Development.

Darling-Hammond, L. (2006). Securing the right to learn: Policy and practice for powerful teaching and learning. *Educational Researcher, 35*(7), 13–24.

Darling-Hammond, L. (2010). *The flat world and education: How America's commitment to equity will determine our future.* New York: Teachers College Press.

Daro, P., Hughes, G. B., & Stancavage, F. (2015). *Study of the alignment of the 2015 NAEP mathematics items at grades 4 and 8 to the Common Core State Standards (CCSS) for mathematics.* Washington, DC: NAEP Validity Studies Panel. Accessed at www.air.org/sites/default/files /downloads/report/Study-of-Alignment-NAEP-Mathematics-Items -common-core-Nov-2015.pdf on October 26, 2015.

DeVault, M. V., & Weaver, J. F. (1970). From settlement to the end of the nineteenth century: 1607–1894. In P. S. Jones & A. F. Coxford Jr. (Eds.), *A history of mathematics education in the United States and Canada* (32nd yearbook, pp. 98–105). Reston, VA: National Council of Teachers of Mathematics.

Dossey, J. A., Halvorsen, K. T., & McCrone, S. S. (in press). *Mathematics education in the United States 2016: A capsule summary fact book.* Reston, VA: National Council for Teachers of Mathematics.

Dweck, C. S. (2006). *Mindset: The new psychology of success.* New York: Random House.

Dweck, C. S. (2008). *Mindsets and math/science achievement.* New York: Carnegie Corporation of New York.

Elementary and Secondary Education Act of 1965, P.L. 89-10, 20 U.S.C. § 6301 (1965).

Every Student Succeeds Act of 2015, P.L. 114-95, 20 U.S.C. § 1177 (2015).

Fernández-Alonso, R., Suárez-Álvarez, J., & Muñiz, J. (2015). Adolescents' homework performance in mathematics and science: Personal factors and teaching practices. *Journal of Educational Psychology.* Accessed at www .apa.org/pubs/journals/releases/edu-0000032.pdf on August 24, 2015.

Fey, J. T., & Graeber, A. O. (2003). From the new math to the Agenda for Action. In G. M. A. Stanic & J. Kilpatrick (Eds.), *A history of school mathematics* (Vol. 1, pp. 521–558). Reston, VA: National Council of Teachers of Mathematics.

Friedman, T. L. (2005). *The world is flat: A brief history of the twenty-first century.* New York: Farrar, Straus and Giroux.

Friedman, T. L., & Mandelbaum, M. (2011). *That used to be us: How America fell behind in the world it invented and how we can come back.* New York: Farrar, Straus and Giroux.

Fuller, B., Wright, J., Gesicki, K., & Kang, E. (2007). Gauging growth: How to judge No Child Left Behind? *Educational Researcher, 36*(5), 268–278.

Fuson, K. C., & Beckmann, S. (2012/2013). Standard algorithms in the Common Core State Standards. *National Council of Supervisors of Mathematics Journal of Mathematics Education Leadership, 14*(2), 4–30.

Fuson, K. C., Kalchman, M., & Bransford, J. D. (2005). Mathematical understanding: An introduction. In M. S. Donovan & J. D. Bransford (Eds.), *How students learn: History, mathematics, and science in the classroom* (pp. 217–256). Washington, DC: National Academies Press.

Garland, S. (2014, March 26). *Why is this Common Core math problem so hard? Supporters respond to quiz that went viral.* Accessed at http://hechingerreport.org/common-core-math-problem on August 24, 2015.

Goodman, M. J., Sands, A. M., & Coley, R. J. (2015, January). *America's skills challenge: Millennials and the future.* Princeton, NJ: Educational Testing Service.

Gullberg, J. (1997). *Mathematics: From the birth of numbers.* New York: W. W. Norton & Company.

Harouni, H. (2015). Toward a political economy of mathematics education. *Harvard Educational Review, 85*(1), 50–74.

Hattie, J. A. C. (2009). *Visible learning: A synthesis of over 800 meta-analyses relating to achievement.* New York: Routledge.

Hattie, J. (2012). *Visible learning for teachers: Maximizing impact on learning.* New York: Routledge.

Heitin, L. (2014, April 21). *Reactions to the 'Common Core' math problem that went viral* [Blog post]. Accessed at http://blogs.edweek.org/edweek/curriculum/2014/04/reactions_to_the_common_core_m.html on August 24, 2015.

Henig, J. R. (2008). *Spin cycle: How research is used in policy debates: The case of charter schools.* New York: Russell Sage Foundation and the Century Foundation.

Herman, J., & Linn, R. (2013, January). *On the road to assessing deeper learning: The status of Smarter Balanced and PARCC assessment consortia* (CRESST Report 823). Los Angeles: University of California, National Center for Research on Evaluation, Standards, and Student Testing.

Hiebert, J. (2013). The constantly underestimated challenge of improving mathematics instruction. In K. R. Leatham (Ed.), *Vital directions for mathematics education research* (pp. 45–56). New York: Springer.

Hiebert, J. S., & Grouws, D. A. (2007). The effects of classroom mathematics teaching on students' learning. In F. K. Lester Jr. (Ed.), *Second handbook of research on mathematics teaching and learning* (pp. 371–404). Charlotte, NC: Information Age.

Jones, P. S., & Coxford, A. F., Jr. (Eds.). (1970). *A history of mathematics education in the United States and Canada* (32nd yearbook). Reston, VA: National Council of Teachers of Mathematics.

Kanold, T. D., Briars, D. J., & Fennell, F. (2012). *What principals need to know about teaching and learning mathematics.* Bloomington, IN: Solution Tree Press.

Kanold, T. D., & Larson, M. (2015). *Beyond the Common Core: A handbook for Mathematics in a PLC at Work™.* Bloomington, IN: Solution Tree Press.

Kertscher, T. (2015, January 16). Scott Walker's shifting position on the common core education standards. *Politifact Wisconsin.* Accessed at www.politifact.com/wisconsin/statements/2015/jan/16/scott-walker/scott -walkers-shifting-position-common-core-educat/ on January 25, 2016.

Kilpatrick, J. (2011). Slouching toward a national curriculum. *Journal of Mathematics Education at Teachers College, 2*(1), 8–17.

Kilpatrick, J. (2014). Mathematics education in the United States and Canada. In A. Karp & G. Schubring (Eds.), *Handbook on the history of mathematics education* (pp. 323–334). New York: Springer.

Kilpatrick, J., Swafford, J., & Findell, B. (Eds.). (2001). *Adding it up: Helping children learn mathematics.* Washington, DC: National Academies Press.

Kisa, M. T., & Stein, M. K. (2015). Learning to see teaching in new ways: A foundation for maintaining cognitive demand. *American Educational Research Journal, 52*(1), 105–136.

Klein, A. (2015, December 10). President signs ESEA rewrite, giving states bigger say on policy. *Education Week.* Accessed at blogs.edweek.org /edweek/campaign-k-12/2015/12/president_barack_obama_signs_e. html on December 10, 2015.

Klein, D. (2003). A brief history of American K–12 mathematics education in the 20th century. In J. M. Royer (Ed.), *Mathematical cognition: A volume in current perspectives on cognition, learning, and instruction* (pp. 175–259). Charlotte, NC: Information Age.

Kline, M. (1973). *Why Johnny can't add: The failure of the new math.* New York: St. Martin's Press.

Kober, N. (1991). *What we know about mathematics teaching and learning.* Washington, DC: Council for Educational Development and Research.

Larson, M. R., & Leinwand, S. (2013a). Prepare for more realistic results. *Teaching Children Mathematics, 19*(9), 533–536.

Larson, M. R., & Leinwand, S. (2013b). Prepare for more realistic testing results. *Mathematics Teaching in the Middle School, 18*(9), 524–526.

Larson, M. R., & Leinwand, S. (2013c). Prepare for more realistic test results. *Mathematics Teacher, 106*(9), 656–659.

Layton, L. (2015, February 17). Christie goes from common core supporter to critic, blames Obama. *The Washington Post.* Accessed at www .washingtonpost.com/local/education/christie-goes-from-common-core -supporter-to-critic-blames-obama/2015/02/17/5e80e66a-b6c4-11e4 -aa05-1ce812b3fdd2_story.html on January 25, 2016.

Leal, F. (2015, October 13). Educators try to come to terms with low math scores on Smarter Balanced tests. *EdSource.* Accessed at www.edsource .org/2015/educators-try-to-come-to-terms-with-low-math-scores-on -smarter-balanced-tests/88899 on January 26, 2016.

Lederman, J., & Kerr, J. C. (2015, October 24). *The big story: Obama encouraging limits on standardized student tests.* Accessed at http:// bigstory.ap.org/article/d819af4dbccb46a3aeea20b7be288f04/obama on October 24, 2015.

Leonard, J., Brooks, W., Barnes-Johnson, J., & Berry, R. Q., III. (2010). The nuances and complexities of teaching mathematics for cultural relevance and social justice. *Journal of Teacher Education, 61*(3), 261–270.

Loveless, T. (2013). *Be wary of ranking NAEP gains.* (Brown Center Chalkboard No. 45). Washington, DC: Brookings Institution. Accessed at www.brookings.edu/research/papers/2013/11/13-interpreting-naep -gains-loveless on October 28, 2015.

Maloney, E. A., Ramirez, G., Gunderson, E. A., Levine, S. C., & Beilock, S. L. (2015). Intergenerational effects of parents' math anxiety on children's math achievement and anxiety. *Psychological Science, 26*(9), 1480–1488.

Martin, D. B. (2007). Beyond missionaries or cannibals: Who should teach mathematics to African American children? *High School Journal, 91*(1), 6–28.

Martin, W. G. (2009). The NCTM high school curriculum project: Why it matters to you. *Mathematics Teacher, 103*(3), 164–166.

Mathews, J. (1972, November 15). New math baffles old mathematician. *The Washington Post*, A1, A13.

Mayer, R. E. (2009). *Multimedia learning* (2nd ed.). New York: Cambridge University Press.

McLeod, D. B. (2003). From consensus to controversy: The story of the NCTM standards. In G. M. A. Stanic & J. Kilpatrick (Eds.), *A history of school mathematics* (Vol. 1, pp. 753–818). Reston, VA: National Council of Teachers of Mathematics.

Michaels, S., O'Connor, C., & Resnick, L. B. (2008). Deliberative discourse idealized and realized: Accountable talk in the classroom and in civic life. *Studies in Philosophy and Education, 27*(4), 283–297.

Moser, J. S., Schroder, H. S., Heeter, C., Moran, T. P., & Lee, Y. (2011). Mind your errors: Evidence for a neural mechanism linking growth mind-set to adaptive posterror adjustments. *Psychological Science, 22*(12), 1444–1484. Accessed at http://pss.sagepub.com/content/22/12/1484 on January 26, 2016.

Munter, C., Stein, M. K., & Smith, M. S. (2015). Dialogic and direct instruction: Two distinct models of mathematics instruction and the debate(s) surrounding them. *Teachers College Record, 117*(11), 1–32.

Mutz, D. C. (2006). *Hearing the other side: Deliberative versus participatory democracy*. New York: Cambridge University Press.

National Center for Education Statistics. (2013). *A first look: 2013 mathematics and reading*. (NCES 2014–451). Washington, DC: Author.

National Center for Education Statistics. (2015). *The nation's report card: 2015 mathematics and reading at grades 4 and 8* (NCES 2015–136). Washington, DC: Author.

National Commission on Excellence in Education. (1983, April). *A nation at risk: The imperative for educational reform*. Washington, DC: U.S. Department of Education.

National Council of Teachers of Mathematics. (1980). *An agenda for action: Recommendations for school mathematics of the 1980s.* Reston, VA: Author.

National Council of Teachers of Mathematics. (1989). *Curriculum and evaluation standards for school mathematics.* Reston, VA: Author.

National Council of Teachers of Mathematics. (1991). *Professional standards for teaching mathematics.* Reston, VA: Author.

National Council of Teachers of Mathematics. (1995). *Assessment standards for school mathematics.* Reston, VA: Author.

National Council of Teachers of Mathematics. (2000). *Principles and standards for school mathematics.* Reston, VA: Author.

National Council of Teachers of Mathematics. (2006). *Curriculum focal points for prekindergarten through grade 8 mathematics: A quest for coherence.* Reston, VA: Author.

National Council of Teachers of Mathematics. (2014). *Principles to actions: Ensuring mathematical success for all.* Reston, VA: Author.

National Education Association. (n.d.). *A parent's guide to helping your child with today's math.* Washington, DC: Author. Accessed at www.nea.org /assets/docs/HE/44013_NEA_W_L9.pdf on December 23, 2015.

National Governors Association Center for Best Practices. (2009). *Forty-nine states and territories join Common Core standards initiative.* Accessed at www.nga.org/cms/home/news-room/news-releases/page_2009/col2 -content/main-content-list/title_forty-nine-states-and-territories-join -common-core-standards-initiative.html on October 7, 2015.

National Governors Association Center for Best Practices & Council of Chief State School Officers. (2010). *Common Core State Standards for mathematics.* Washington, DC: Authors. Accessed at www.corestandards .org/assets/CCSSI_Math%20Standards.pdf on November 22, 2010.

National Mathematics Advisory Panel. (2008, March). *Foundations for success: The final report of the National Mathematics Advisory Panel.* Washington, DC: U.S. Department of Education.

National Research Council. (2012a). *Education for life and work: Developing transferable knowledge and skills in the 21st century.* Washington, DC: The National Academies Press.

National Research Council. (2012b). *Fueling innovation and discovery: The mathematical sciences in the 21st century.* Washington, DC: The National Academies Press.

No Child Left Behind Act of 2001, P.L. 107–110, 20 U.S.C. § 6319 (2002).

Organisation for Economic Co-operation and Development. (2014). *PISA 2012 results in focus: What 15-year-olds know and what they can do with what they know.* Paris: Author.

Pariser, E. (2011). *The filter bubble: How the new personalized web is changing what we read and how we think.* New York: Penguin.

Pashler, H., Bain, P. M., Bottge, B. A., Graesser, A., Koedinger, K., McDaniel, M., et al. (2007, September). *Organizing instruction and study to improve student learning: A practice guide* (NCER 2007–2004). Washington, DC: National Center for Education Research, Institute of Education Sciences, U.S. Department of Education.

Peterson, P., & Ackerman, M. (2015). States raise proficiency standards in math and reading. *Education Next, 15*(3). 16–21. Accessed at http:// educationnext.org/files/ednext_XV_3_peterson.pdf on February 2, 2016.

Peterson, P., Barrows, S., & Gift, T. (2016). After Common Core, states set rigorous standards. *Education Next, 16*(3), 1–9. Accessed at http:// educationnext.org/after-common-core-states-set-rigorous-standards/ on January 28, 2016.

Phillips, C. J. (2015). *The new math: A political history.* Chicago: University of Chicago Press.

Phillips, G. W. (2010, October). *International benchmarking: State education performance standards.* Washington, DC: American Institutes for Research.

Pike, N. (1788). *A new and complete system of arithmetic, composed for the use of the citizens of the United States.* Newburyport, MA: Mycall.

Porter, A., McMaken, J., Hwang, J., & Yang, R. (2011). Common Core standards: The new U.S. intended curriculum. *Educational Researcher, 40*(3), 103–116.

Qiu, L. (2015, June 8). Bobby Jindal's change of position on Common Core. *Politifact.* Accessed at www.politifact.com/truth-o-meter /statements/2015/jun/08/bobby-jindal/bobby-jindal-change-position -common-core/ on January 25, 2016.

Reeves, D. (2011). *Elements of grading: A guide to effective practice.* Bloomington, IN: Solution Tree Press.

Riffkin, R. (2014, August 28). *America's satisfaction with education system increases.* Accessed at www.gallup.com/poll/175517/americans -satisfaction-education-system-increases.aspx on August 30, 2014.

Ripley, A. (2013). *The smartest kids in the world: And how they got that way.* New York: Simon & Schuster.

Roodhouse, E. A. (2009). The voice from the base(ment): Stridency, referential structure, and partisan conformity in the political blogosphere. *First Monday, 14*(9). Accessed at http://firstmonday.org/ojs /index.php/fm/article/view/2624/2289 on January 12, 2016.

Schmidt, W. H. (2012). Seizing the moment for mathematics. *Education Week, 31*(36), 24–25.

Schmidt, W. H., Cogan, L. S., Houang, R. T., & McKnight, C. C. (2011). Content coverage differences across districts/states: A persisting challenge for U.S. education policy. *American Journal of Education, 117*(3), 399–427.

Schmidt, W. H., & Houang, R. T. (2012). Curricular coherence and the Common Core State Standards for mathematics. *Educational Researcher, 41*(8), 294–308.

Silver, E. (2010). Examining what teachers do when they display their best practice: Teaching mathematics for understanding. *Journal of Mathematics Education at Teachers College, 1*(1), 1–6.

Smith, M. S., & Stein, M. K. (2012). Selecting and creating mathematical tasks: From research to practice. In G. Lappan, M. S. Smith, & E. Jones (Eds.), *Rich and engaging mathematical tasks, grades 5–9* (pp. 344–350). Reston, VA: National Council of Teachers of Mathematics.

Stein, M. K., Remillard, J., & Smith, M. S. (2007). How curriculum influences student learning. In F. K. Lester Jr. (Ed.), *Second handbook of research on mathematics teaching and learning* (pp. 319–370). Charlotte, NC: Information Age.

Stigler, J. W., & Hiebert, J. (1999). *The teaching gap: Best ideas from the world's teachers for improving education in the classroom.* New York: Free Press.

Stigler, J. W., & Thompson, B. J. (2009). Thoughts on creating, accumulating, and utilizing shareable knowledge to improve teaching. *Elementary School Journal, 109*(5), 442–457.

Supovitz, J., Daly, A., & del Fresno, M. (n.d.). *#commoncore: How social media is changing the politics of education.* Accessed at www .hashtagcommoncore.com on March 17, 2015.

Thames, M. H., & Ball, D. L. (2013). Making progress in U.S. mathematics education: Lessons learned—past, present, and future. In K. R. Leatham (Ed.), *Vital directions for mathematics education research* (pp. 15–44). New York: Springer.

Thorndike, E. L. (1922). *The psychology of arithmetic.* New York: Macmillan.

Ujifusa, A. (2015, December 15). National graduation rate increased to all-time high of 82 percent. *Education Week.* Accessed at blogs.edweek .org/edweek/campaign-k-12/2015/12/national_graduation_rate_incre .html?cmp=eml-eml-eu-news2 on December 15, 1015.

U.S. Department of Education. (2005). *Helping your child learn mathematics.* Washington, DC: Author. Accessed at www2.ed.gov /parents/academic/help/math/math.pdf on August 24, 2015.

Walsh, J. A., & Sattes, B. D. (2005). *Quality questioning: Research-based practice to engage every learner.* Thousand Oaks, CA: Corwin Press.

Warshauer, H. K. (2011). *The role of productive struggle in teaching and learning middle school mathematics.* Doctoral dissertation, University of Texas at Austin.

West, D. M., Whitehurst, G. J., & Dionne, E. J., Jr. (2011, March). *Americans want more coverage of teacher performance and student achievement.* Washington, DC: Brookings Institution.

Whitenack, J. W., Cavey, L. O., & Henney, C. (2015). *It's elementary: A parent's guide to K–5 mathematics.* Reston, VA: National Council of Teachers of Mathematics.

Wu, H. (1999). Basic skills versus conceptual understanding: A bogus dichotomy in mathematics education. *American Educator, 23*(3), 1–7.

Wu, H. (2011). *Understanding numbers in elementary school mathematics.* Providence, RI: American Mathematical Society.

Yettick, H. (2015). One small droplet: News media coverage of peer-reviewed and university-based education research and academic expertise. *Educational Researcher, 44*(3), 173–184.

Zacharias, M. (Producer). (2009). *Math: What's the problem?* [Flash multimedia presentation]. Accessed at www.nsf.gov/news/special _reports/math on August 24, 2015.

Zinshteyn, M. (2015, January 12). *Black and Hispanic students are making meaningful gains, but it's hard to tell.* Accessed at http://fivethirtyeight .com/features/black-and-hispanic-students-are-making-meaningful -gains-but-its-hard-to-tell on August 24, 2015.

Index

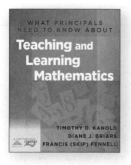

What Principals Need to Know About Teaching and Learning Mathematics
Timothy D. Kanold, Diane J. Briars, and Francis (Skip) Fennell

This must-have resource offers support and encouragement for improved mathematics achievement and covers the importance of mathematics content, learning and instruction, and assessment.

BKF501

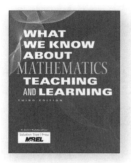

What We Know About Mathematics Teaching and Learning, 3rd Edition
McREL

Designed for accessibility, this book supports mathematics education reform and brings the rich world of education research and practice to preK–12 educators.

BKF395

It's TIME
The National Council of Supervisors of Mathematics

Discover best practices to fully align curriculum with the CCSS for mathematics, and gain practical strategies for supporting mathematics learning.

BKF600

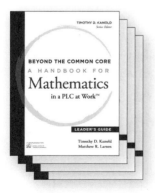

Beyond the Common Core series
Edited by Timothy D. Kanold

Designed to go beyond the content of state standards, this series offers an action-oriented guide for focusing mathematics instruction to positively impact student achievement.

BKF627, BKF628, BKF626, BKF634

> I came to the presentation pretty much devoid of an understanding of how the **Common Core** was going to affect my students and my instructional methods. I walked away **excited** and feeling **validated.**
>
> # I'm on board!

—David Nohe, teacher,
New Mexico School for the Blind and Visually Impaired

PD Services

Our experts draw from decades of research and their own experiences to bring you practical strategies for integrating the Common Core. You can choose from a range of customizable services, from a one-day overview to a multiyear process.

Book your CCSS PD today!
888.763.9045

Solution Tree

Solution Tree

Solution Tree's mission is to advance the work of our authors. By working with the best researchers and educators worldwide, we strive to be the premier provider of innovative publishing, in-demand events, and inspired professional development designed to transform education to ensure that all students learn.

NATIONAL COUNCIL OF
TEACHERS OF MATHEMATICS

The National Council of Teachers of Mathematics is the public voice of mathematics education, supporting teachers to ensure equitable mathematics learning of the highest quality for all students through vision, leadership, professional development, and research.